Microsoft®
WINDOWS VISTA
Simplified®

Visual®

by Paul McFedries

Wiley Publishing, Inc.

Microsoft®
WINDOWS VISTA™
SIMPLIFIED®

Published by
Wiley Publishing, Inc.
111 River Street
Hoboken, NJ 07030-5774

Published simultaneously in Canada

Library of Congress Control Number: 2006937058

ISBN: 978-0-470-04575-6

Manufactured in the United States of America

10 9 8 7 6 5 4 3 2

Contact Us

For general information on our other products and services please contact our Customer Care Department within the U.S. at 800-762-2974, outside the U.S. at 317-572-3993, or fax 317-572-4002.

For technical support please visit www.wiley.com/techsupport.

In order to get this information to you in a timely manner, this book was based on a prerelease version of Microsoft Windows Vista. There may be some minor changes between the screenshots in this book and what you see on your desktop. As always, Microsoft has the final word on how programs look and function; if you have any questions or see any discrepancies, consult the online help for further information about the software.

WILEY

Wiley Publishing, Inc.

Sales

Contact Wiley
at (800) 762-2974 or
fax (317) 572-4002.

Praise for Visual Books

"Like a lot of other people, I understand things best when I see them visually. Your books really make learning easy and life more fun."

John T. Frey (Cadillac, MI)

"I have quite a few of your Visual books and have been very pleased with all of them. I love the way the lessons are presented!"

Mary Jane Newman (Yorba Linda, CA)

"I just purchased my third Visual book (my first two are dog-eared now!), and, once again, your product has surpassed my expectations."

Tracey Moore (Memphis, TN)

"I am an avid fan of your Visual books. If I need to learn anything, I just buy one of your books and learn the topic in no time. Wonders! I have even trained my friends to give me Visual books as gifts."

Illona Bergstrom (Aventura, FL)

"Thank you for making it so clear. I appreciate it. I will buy many more Visual books."

J.P. Sangdong (North York, Ontario, Canada)

"I have several books from the Visual series and have always found them to be valuable resources."

Stephen P. Miller (Ballston Spa, NY)

"Thank you for the wonderful books you produce. It wasn't until I was an adult that I discovered how I learn — visually. Nothing compares to Visual books. I love the simple layout. I can just grab a book and use it at my computer, lesson by lesson. And I understand the material! You really know the way I think and learn. Thanks so much!"

Stacey Han (Avondale, AZ)

"I absolutely admire your company's work. Your books are terrific. The format is perfect, especially for visual learners like me. Keep them coming!"

Frederick A. Taylor, Jr. (New Port Richey, FL)

"I have several of your Visual books and they are the best I have ever used."

Stanley Clark (Crawfordville, FL)

"I bought my first Visual book last month. Wow. Now I want to learn everything in this easy format!"

Tom Vial (New York, NY)

"Thank you, thank you, thank you...for making it so easy for me to break into this high-tech world. I now own four of your books. I recommend them to anyone who is a beginner like myself."

Gay O'Donnell (Calgary, Alberta, Canada)

"I write to extend my thanks and appreciation for your books. They are clear, easy to follow, and straight to the point. Keep up the good work! I bought several of your books and they are just right! No regrets! I will always buy your books because they are the best."

Seward Kollie (Dakar, Senegal)

"Compliments to the chef!! Your books are extraordinary! Or, simply put, extra-ordinary, meaning way above the rest! THANK YOU THANK YOU THANK YOU! I buy them for friends, family, and colleagues."

Christine J. Manfrin (Castle Rock, CO)

"What fantastic teaching books you have produced! Congratulations to you and your staff. You deserve the Nobel Prize in Education in the Software category. Thanks for helping me understand computers."

Bruno Tonon (Melbourne, Australia)

"Over time, I have bought a number of your 'Read Less - Learn More' books. For me, they are THE way to learn anything easily. I learn easiest using your method of teaching."

José A. Mazón (Cuba, NY)

"I am an avid purchaser and reader of the Visual series, and they are the greatest computer books I've seen. The Visual books are perfect for people like myself who enjoy the computer, but want to know how to use it more efficiently. Your books have definitely given me a greater understanding of my computer, and have taught me to use it more effectively. Thank you very much for the hard work, effort, and dedication that you put into this series."

Alex Diaz (Las Vegas, NV)

Credits

Project Editor
Kim Heusel

Acquisitions Editor
Jody Lefevere

Product Development Supervisor
Courtney Allen

Copy Editor
Lauren Kennedy

Technical Editor
Don Passenger

Editorial Manager
Robyn Siesky

Editorial Assistant
Laura Sinise

Business Manager
Amy Knies

Manufacturing
Allan Conley
Linda Cook
Paul Gilchrist
Jennifer Guynn

Book Design
Kathie Rickard

Production Coordinator
Adrienne Martinez

Layout
Elizabeth Brooks
LeAndra Hosier
Jennifer Mayberry

Screen Artist
Jill A. Proll

Illustrators
Ronda David-Burroughs
Cheryl Grubbs

Proofreader
Sossity R. Smith

Quality Control
Laura Albert
John Greenough
Susan Moritz

Indexer
Johnna VanHoose

Vice President and Executive Group Publisher
Richard Swadley

Vice President and Publisher
Barry Pruett

Composition Director
Debbie Stailey

About the Author

Paul McFedries is the president of Logophilia Limited, a technical writing company. While now primarily a writer, Paul has worked as a programmer, consultant, and Web site developer. Paul has written more than 50 books that have sold over three million copies worldwide. These books include the Wiley titles *Windows Vista: Top 100 Simplified Tips and Trick*; *The Unofficial Guide to Microsoft Office 2007*; and *Teach Yourself VISUALLY Computers*, 4th Edition. Paul also runs Word Spy, a Web site dedicated to tracking new words and phrases (see www.wordspy.com).

Author's Acknowledgments

The book you hold in your hands is not only an excellent learning tool, but it is truly beautiful, as well. I am happy to have supplied the text that you will read, but the gorgeous images come from Wiley's crack team of artists and illustrators. The layout of the tasks, the accuracy of the spelling and grammar, and the veracity of the information are all the result of hard work performed by project editor Kim Heusel, copy editor Lauren Kennedy, and technical editor Don Passenger. Thanks to all of you for your excellent work. My thanks, as well, to acquisitions editor Jody Lefevere for bringing me onboard, and to publisher Barry Pruett for recommending me.

Table of Contents

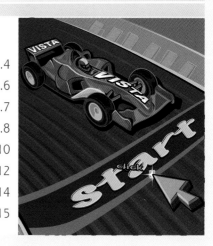

3

Creating and Editing Documents

4

Working with Images

Table of Contents

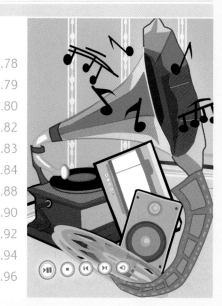

7

Sharing Your Computer with Others

8

Surfing the World Wide Web

Table of Contents

9

10

Chapter 1

Getting Started with Windows Vista

Are you ready to learn about Windows Vista? In this chapter, you learn the basics of starting and activating Windows Vista, getting help, and shutting down your system.

Start
Windows Vista

When you turn on your computer, Windows Vista starts automatically, but you may have to navigate the Welcome screen along the way.

The first time you start your computer, you may need to run through a series of configuration steps.

Start Windows Vista

1 Turn on your computer.

● The Windows Vista Welcome screen appears.

> **Note:** *If your version of Windows Vista is configured with just a single user and no password, then you will bypass the Welcome screen and go directly to the desktop.*

2 Click the icon that corresponds to your Windows Vista user name.

Windows Vista may ask you to enter your password.

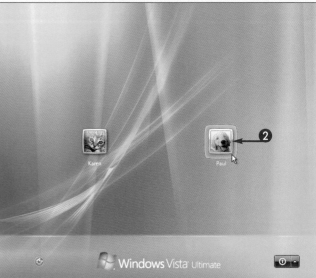

③ Type your password.

Note: *The password characters appear as dots as you type them so that no one else can read your password.*

④ Click the **Go** arrow ().

The Windows Vista desktop appears.

What happens if I forget my Windows Vista password?
Most Windows Vista user accounts that are password protected are also set up with a password "hint" — usually a word or phrase designed to jog your memory. You choose the question when you set your password, as explained in the "Protect an Account with a Password" task in Chapter 7. If you forget your password, click the **Go** arrow () and then click **OK** to see the password hint.

What You Can Do with Windows Vista

Windows Vista is an operating system that contains a collection of tools, programs, and resources. Here is a sampling of what you can do with them.

Get Work Done

With Windows Vista, you can run programs that enable you to get your work done more efficiently, such as a word processor for writing memos and letters, a spreadsheet for making calculations, and a database for storing information. Windows Vista comes with some of these programs (such as the WordPad program you learn about in Chapter 3), and there are others you can purchase and install separately.

Create and Edit Pictures

Windows Vista comes with a lot of features that let you work with images. You can create your own pictures from scratch, import images from a scanner or digital camera, or download images from the Internet. After you create or acquire an image, you can edit it, print it, or send it via e-mail. You learn about these and other picture tasks in Chapter 4.

Play Music and Other Media

Windows Vista has treats for your ears as well as your eyes. You can listen to audio CDs, play digital sound and video clips, watch DVD movies, tune in to Internet radio stations, and copy audio files to a recordable CD. You learn about these multimedia tasks in Chapter 5.

Get on the Internet

Windows Vista makes connecting to the Internet easy (see Chapter 9). And after you are on the Net, Windows Vista has all the tools you need to get the most out of your experience. For example, you can use Internet Explorer to surf the World Wide Web (see Chapter 10) and Windows Mail to send and receive e-mail (see Chapter 11).

The Windows Vista Screen

Before getting to the specifics of working with Windows Vista, take a few seconds to familiarize yourself with the basic screen elements.

Desktop Icon
An icon on the desktop represents a program or Windows Vista feature. A program you install often adds its own icon on the desktop.

Mouse Pointer
When you move your mouse, this pointer moves along with it.

Desktop
This is the Windows Vista ìwork area," meaning that it is where you work with your programs and documents.

Time
This is the current time on your computer. To see the current date, position the mouse ⌖ over the time. To change the date or time, double-click the time.

Notification Area
This area displays small icons that notify you about things that are happening on your computer. For example, you see notifications if your printer runs out of paper or if an update to Windows Vista is available over the Internet.

Start Button
You use this button to start programs and launch many of Windows Vista's features.

Quick Launch Toolbar
You use these icons to launch some Windows Vista features with just a mouse click.

Taskbar
The programs you have open appear in the taskbar. You use this area to switch between programs if you have more than one running at a time.

Using a Mouse with Windows Vista

Windows Vista was built with the mouse in mind, so it pays to learn the basic mouse techniques early on, because you will use them throughout your Windows career.

If you have never used a mouse before, this approach to learning how to use it is key: Keep all your movements slow and deliberate, and practice the techniques in this task as much as you can.

Using a Mouse with Windows Vista

CLICK THE MOUSE

 Position the mouse ⬚ over the object with which you want to work.

 Click the left mouse button.

● Depending on the object, Windows Vista either selects the object or performs some operation in response to the click (such as displaying the Start menu).

DOUBLE-CLICK THE MOUSE

 Move the mouse ⬚ over the object with which you want to work.

 Click the left mouse button twice in quick succession.

● Windows Vista usually performs some operation in response to the double-click action (such as displaying the Recycle Bin window).

RIGHT-CLICK THE MOUSE

1 Position the mouse ⌖ over the object with which you want to work.

2 Click the right mouse button.

● Windows Vista displays a shortcut menu when you right-click something.

Note: *The contents of the shortcut menu depends on the object you right-clicked.*

CLICK AND DRAG THE MOUSE

1 Position the mouse ⌖ over the object with which you want to work.

2 Click and hold the left mouse button.

3 Move the mouse to drag the selected object.

● In most cases, the object moves along with the mouse ⌖.

4 Release the mouse button when the selected object is repositioned.

Why does Windows Vista sometimes not recognize my double-clicks?
Try to double-click as quickly as you can, and be sure not to move the mouse between clicks. If you continue to have trouble, click **Start**, **Control Panel**, and then **Mouse** to open the Mouse Properties dialog box. In the Double-click speed group, click and drag the slider to the left (toward Slow).

How can I set up my mouse for a left-hander?
Click **Start**, **Control Panel**, and then **Mouse** to open the Mouse Properties dialog box. Click **Switch primary and secondary buttons** (☐ changes to ☑).

Get Help

Most of the Help system is arranged into various topics, such as "Get pictures from your camera" and "Make your computer battery last longer." Each topic offers a number of subtopics, and each subtopic contains a collection of related tasks, articles, tutorials, and other items.

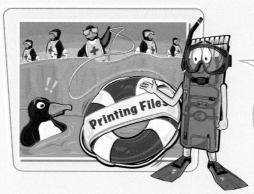

You can find out more about Windows Vista, learn how to perform a task, or troubleshoot problems by accessing the Help system.

Get Help

① Click **Start**.

The Start menu appears.

② Click **Help and Support**.

● The Windows Help and Support window appears.

③ Click the **Table of Contents** button.

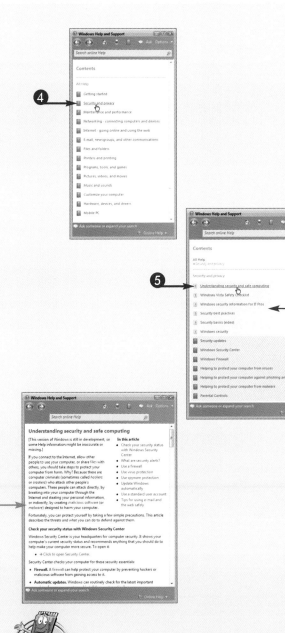

The Table of Contents appears.

④ Click a topic.

● A list of Help articles appears for the topic you selected.

● A list of subtopics appears for the topic you selected.

⑤ Click an article, task, an overview, or a tutorial.

Note: *If the article you want is part of a subtopic, click the subtopic to display the list of articles it contains, and then click the article.*

● The item you select appears in the Help and Support Center window.

⑥ Read the article.

Note: *To return to a previous Help and Support Center screen, click the* **Back** *button (⬅) until you get to the screen you want.*

How do I get help for a specific program?

Almost all Windows programs have their own Help features. You can access Help in a specific program one of three main ways:

● Click **Help** from the menu, and then click the command that runs the Help features (it may be called **Help Contents**, **Help Topics**, or **Program Help**, where *Program* is the name of the program (for example, **Microsoft Word Help**).

● Press **F1**.

● In a dialog box, click the **Help** button (?), and then click a control to see a description of the control.

Activate Your Copy
of Windows Vista

To avoid piracy, Microsoft requires that each copy of Windows Vista be activated. Otherwise, your copy of Windows Vista will refuse to run after the activation period has expired.

This task assumes that Windows Vista has not yet prompted you to start the activation. If you see an icon in the notification area with the message "Activate Windows now," click that message and then skip to Step 5.

Activate Your Copy of Windows Vista

1 Click **Start**.

2 Right-click **Computer**.

3 Click **Properties**.

The System window appears.

Note: If the System window shows the Ask for Genuine Microsoft Software logo in the Windows Activation area, then you do not need to perform the rest of the steps in this task. Click the **Close** button ([X]) to close the System window.

4 Click the **Automatic activation will begin in X days. Click here to activate Windows now** link.

Note: If the User Account Control dialog box appears, click **Continue** or type an administrator password and click **Submit**.

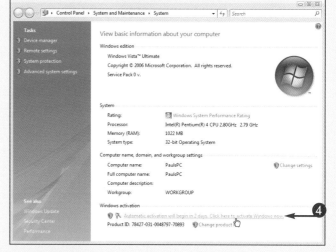

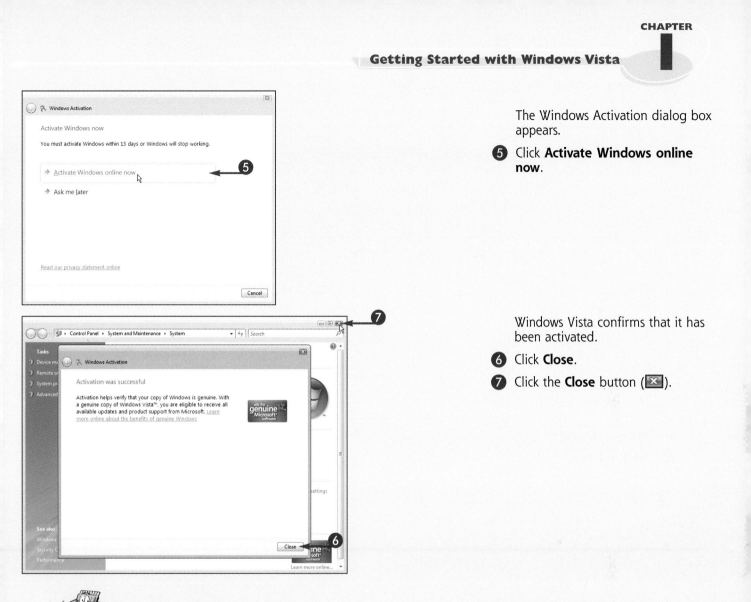

The Windows Activation dialog box appears.

⑤ Click **Activate Windows online now**.

Windows Vista confirms that it has been activated.

⑥ Click **Close**.

⑦ Click the **Close** button (⊠).

Can I activate Windows Vista on more than one computer?
No, not usually. The activation process creates a special value that is unique to your computer's hardware configuration. When you activate Windows Vista, your copy of the program is associated with this unique hardware value, which means your copy only works with that one computer. However, if that computer breaks down, you can telephone Microsoft to let them know, and they should allow you to activate Vista on another computer.

How can I activate my copy of Windows Vista if I do not have Internet access?
If you do not have Internet access, perform Steps **1** to **5** anyway. After a few moments, Windows Activation displays a list of options. Click **Show me other ways to activate**. If your computer has a modem attached, click **Use my modem to connect directly to the activation service**. If you do not have a modem, click **Use the automated phone system**, instead.

13

Restart Windows Vista

Knowing how to restart Windows Vista also comes in handy when you install a program or device that requires a restart to function properly. If you are busy right now, you can always opt to restart your computer yourself later, when it is more convenient.

You can restart Windows Vista, which means it shuts down and starts up again immediately. This is useful if your computer is running slow or acting funny. Sometimes a restart solves the problem.

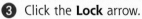

Restart Windows Vista

① Shut down all your running programs.

Note: *Be sure to save your work as you close your programs.*

② Click **Start**.

● The Start menu appears.

③ Click the **Lock** arrow.

● The Lock menu appears.

④ Click **Restart**.

Windows Vista shuts down and your computer restarts.

Shut Down Windows Vista

Shutting off the computer's power without properly exiting Windows Vista can cause two problems. First, if you have unsaved changes in some open documents, you may lose those changes. Second, you could damage one or more Windows Vista system files, which could make your system unstable.

When you complete your work for the day, you should shut down Windows Vista. However, do not just shut off your computer's power. Follow the proper steps to avoid damaging files on your system.

Shut Down Windows Vista

① Shut down all your running programs.

   Note: Be sure to save your work as you close your programs.

② Click **Start**.

   ● The Start menu appears.

③ Click the **Lock** arrow.

   ● The Lock menu appears.

④ Click **Shut Down**.

   Windows Vista shuts down and turns off your computer.

   ● If you want Windows Vista to automatically reopen all the programs and documents currently on your screen, click the **Sleep** button ( ), instead.

Chapter 2

Launching and Working with Programs

On its own, Windows Vista does not do very much. To do something useful with your computer, you need to work with a program, either one that comes with Windows Vista or one that you install yourself. In this chapter, you learn how to install, launch, and work with programs.

Install a Program

Install a Program

If Windows Vista does not come with a program that you need, you can obtain the program yourself and then install it on your computer.

How you start the installation process depends on whether the program comes on a CD, a DVD, or a floppy disk, or from the Internet.

INSTALL FROM A CD OR DVD

① Insert the program's CD or DVD into the appropriate disk drive.

● The AutoPlay dialog box appears.

   Note: *If the AutoPlay dialog box does not appear after you insert the disc, see the instructions in the "Install from a Floppy Disk" section of this task.*

② Click **Run file**, where *file* is the name of the installation program (usually setup.EXE).

③ Follow the installation instructions the program provides.

   Note: *Installation steps vary from program to program.*

INSTALL FROM A FILE DOWNLOADED FROM THE INTERNET

① Use Windows Explorer to find the downloaded file.

   Note: *To view a file with Windows Explorer, see the "View Your Files" task in Chapter 6.*

② Double-click the file.

   The software's installation program begins.

   Note: *For compressed files, extract the files, and then double-click the setup file. See the "Extract Files from a Compressed Folder" task in Chapter 6.*

③ Follow the installation instructions the program provides.

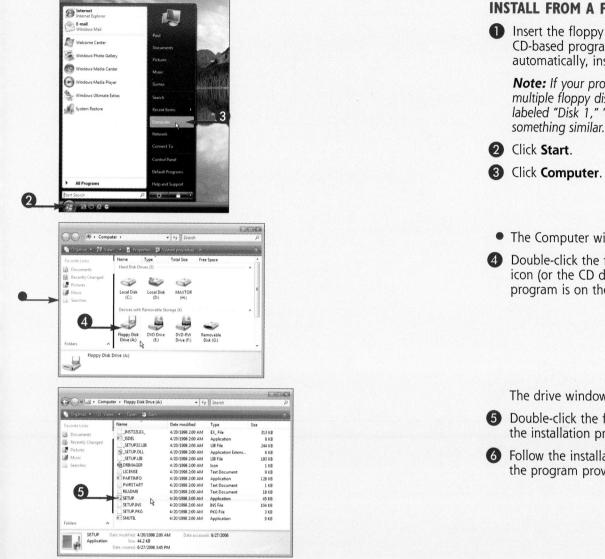

INSTALL FROM A FLOPPY DISK

1 Insert the floppy disk or, if your CD-based program does not install automatically, insert the CD.

> **Note:** If your program comes on multiple floppy disks, insert the disk labeled "Disk 1," "Setup," or something similar.

2 Click **Start**.

3 Click **Computer**.

● The Computer window appears.

4 Double-click the floppy disk drive icon (or the CD drive icon if the program is on the CD).

The drive window appears.

5 Double-click the file that launches the installation program.

6 Follow the installation instructions the program provides.

How do I find my software's product key or serial number?

The product key or serial number is crucial because many programs will not install until you enter the number. Look for a sticker attached to the back or inside of the CD case. Also look on the registration card, the CD itself, or the back of the box. If you downloaded the program, the number should appear on the download screen and on the e-mail receipt you receive.

Change or Repair a Program Installation

When you install a program, you can choose the "custom" installation option to install only some of the program's components. If you decide later on to install more components or remove installed components, you can rerun the install program to make these changes.

If an installed program will not start or is behaving erratically, it may have one or more missing or corrupt files. Many programs come with a repair option that can fix such problems.

Change or Repair a Program Installation

① Click **Start**.

② Click **Control Panel**.

The Control Panel window appears.

③ Click **Uninstall a program**.

The Programs and Features window appears.

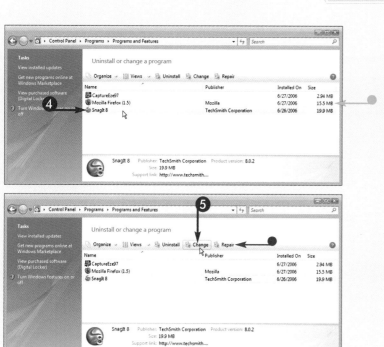

● Windows Vista displays a list of the programs installed on your computer.

④ Click the program with which you want to work.

⑤ Click **Change**.

Note: For some programs, you click **Uninstall/Change**, instead.

● If you want to repair the program, click **Repair** instead.

⑥ Follow the installation instructions the program provides.

What is the difference between a "typical" and "custom" installation?

A "typical" installation automatically installs only those program components that people use most often. In a "custom" installation, you select which components are installed, where they are installed, and so on. The custom option is best suited for experienced users, so you are usually better off choosing the typical install.

Start a Program

To work with any program, you must first tell Windows Vista which program you want to run. Windows Vista then launches the program and displays it on the desktop.

Start a Program

1 Click **Start**.

The Start menu appears.

2 Click **All Programs**.

● After you click All Programs, the name changes to Back.

The All Programs menu appears.

3 Click the icon for the program you want to launch.

● If your program icon is in a submenu, click the submenu and then click the program icon.

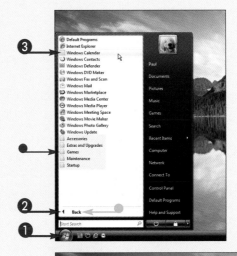

The program appears on the desktop.

● Windows Vista adds a button for the program to the taskbar.

Note: *After you have used a program a few times, it may appear on the main Start menu. If so, you can launch the program by clicking its Start menu icon.*

Understanding Program Windows

You work with a program by manipulating the various features of its window.

System Menu Icon
Clicking this icon displays a menu that enables you to work with program windows via the keyboard.

Title Bar
The title bar displays the name of the program. In some programs, the title bar also displays the name of the open document. You can also use the title bar to move the window.

Menu Bar
The menu bar contains the pull-down menus for Windows Vista and most Windows Vista software. In some programs you must press Alt to see the menu bar.

Toolbar
Buttons that offer easy access to common program commands and features appear in the toolbar. Some buttons are commands and some have lists from which you can make a choice.

Minimize Button
You click Minimize ( ) to remove the window from the desktop and display only the window's taskbar button. The window is still open, but not active.

Close Button
When you click Close ( ), the program shuts down.

Maximize Button
To enlarge the window either from the taskbar or so that it takes up the entire desktop, you click Maximize ( ).

Using Pull-Down Menus

When you are ready to work with a program, use the pull-down menus to access the program's commands and features.

The items in a pull-down menu are either commands that execute some action in the program, or features that you turn on and off. If you do not see any menus, you can often display them by pressing Alt.

Using Pull-Down Menus

RUN COMMANDS

1. Click the name of the menu you want to display.

● The program displays the menu.

You can also display a menu by holding down Alt and pressing the underlined letter in the menu name.

2. Click the command you want to run.

The program runs the command.

● If your command is in a submenu, click the submenu and then click the desired command.

TURN FEATURES ON AND OFF

1. Click the name of the menu you want to display.

● The program displays the menu.

2. Click the menu item.

Click a submenu if your command is not on the main menu.

● Toggle features are either turned on (indicated by ☑) or off (no check mark appears).

● Click an option feature to turn it on (indicated by ⦿) and turn off the previously activated item.

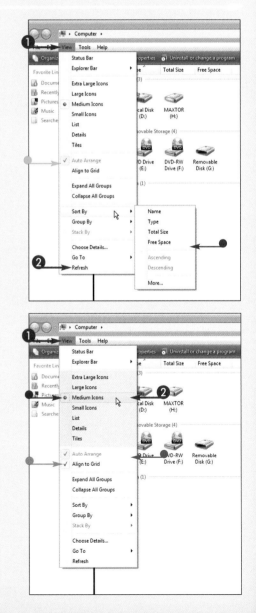

Using Toolbars

You can use the toolbar to access commands faster than using the menus. Most programs come with one or more toolbars, which are collections of buttons that in most cases give you one-click access to the program's most common features.

Using Toolbars

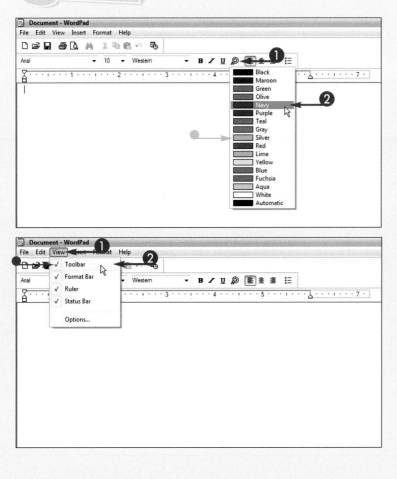

❶ Click the toolbar button that represents the command or list.

Note: If the toolbar button remains "pressed" after you click it, the button toggles a feature on and off and the feature is now on. To turn the feature off, click the button to "unpress" it.

● The program executes the command or, as shown here, drops down the list.

❷ If a list appears, click the list item that represents the command.

The program runs the command.

DISPLAY AND HIDE TOOLBARS

❶ Click **View**.

❷ Click **Toolbar**.

● If the toolbar is currently displayed (indicated by ☑ in the View menu), the program hides the toolbar.

If the toolbar is currently hidden, the program displays the toolbar (indicated by ☑ in the View menu).

Note: Some programs can display multiple toolbars. In this case, you click View, Toolbars, and then click the toolbar you want to display or hide.

Understanding
Dialog Box Controls

Dialog boxes appear when a program needs you to provide information. You provide that information by manipulating various types of controls.

Option Button

Clicking an option button turns on a program feature. Only one option button in a group can be turned on at a time. When you click an option button, it changes from ◎ to ◉.

Tab

The various tabs in a dialog box display different sets of controls. You can choose from these settings in a dialog box to achieve a variety of results.

Check Box

Clicking a check box toggles a program feature on and off. If you are turning a feature on, the check box changes from ☐ to ☑; if you are turning the feature off, the check box changes from ☑ to ☐.

Combo Box

The combo box combines both a text box and a list box.

Drop-Down List Box

A drop-down list box displays only the selected item from a list. You can open the list to select a different item.

Spin Button

The spin button (⬍) enables you to choose a numeric value.

List Box

A list box displays a list of items from which you can select a relatively large number of choices. There are various types of lists, and you need to know how to use them all.

Text Box

A text box enables you to enter typed text.

Command Button

Clicking a command button executes the command written on the button face. For example, you can click **OK** to put settings you choose in a dialog box into effect, or you can click **Cancel** to close the dialog box without changing the settings.

Using Dialog Boxes

For example, when you print a document, you use the Print dialog box to specify the number of copies you want printed.

You use dialog boxes to control how a program works. Dialog boxes appear frequently, so you need to know how to use them to get the most out of any program.

Using Dialog Boxes

USING A TEXT BOX

1 Click inside the text box.

● A blinking, vertical bar (called a *cursor* or an *insertion point*) appears inside the text box.

2 Use **Backspace** or **Delete** to delete any existing characters.

3 Type your text.

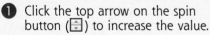

ENTER A VALUE WITH A SPIN BUTTON

1 Click the top arrow on the spin button (⬍) to increase the value.

2 Click the bottom arrow on the spin button (⬍) to decrease the value.

● You can also type the value in the text box.

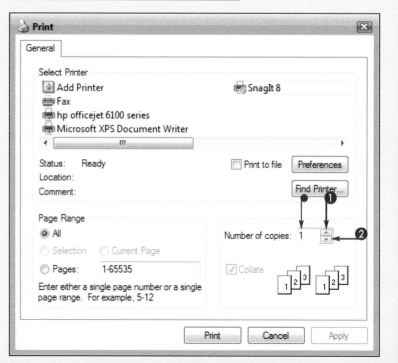

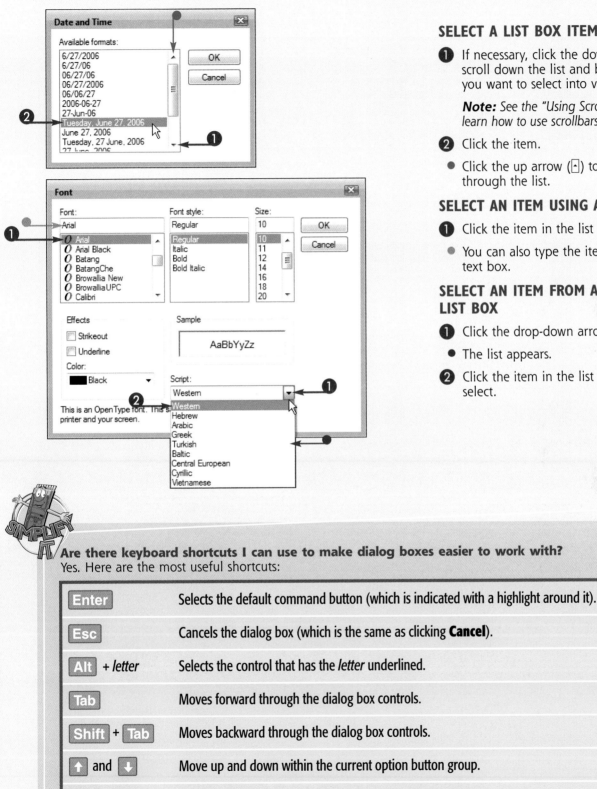

SELECT A LIST BOX ITEM

1. If necessary, click the down arrow (▾) to scroll down the list and bring the item you want to select into view.

   Note: See the "Using Scrollbars" task to learn how to use scrollbars.

2. Click the item.

   ● Click the up arrow (▴) to scroll back up through the list.

SELECT AN ITEM USING A COMBO BOX

1. Click the item in the list box to select it.

   ● You can also type the item name in the text box.

SELECT AN ITEM FROM A DROP-DOWN LIST BOX

1. Click the drop-down arrow (▾).

   ● The list appears.

2. Click the item in the list that you want to select.

Are there keyboard shortcuts I can use to make dialog boxes easier to work with?
Yes. Here are the most useful shortcuts:

Enter	Selects the default command button (which is indicated with a highlight around it).
Esc	Cancels the dialog box (which is the same as clicking **Cancel**).
Alt + *letter*	Selects the control that has the *letter* underlined.
Tab	Moves forward through the dialog box controls.
Shift + Tab	Moves backward through the dialog box controls.
↑ and ↓	Move up and down within the current option button group.
Alt + ↓	Drops down the selected combo box or drop-down list box.

Work with
Program Windows

For example, you can minimize a window to clear it from the desktop. Similarly, you can move or resize windows so that they do not overlap each other.

You need to know how to work with program windows so that you can keep your desktop neat and your programs easier to find.

Work with Program Windows

MINIMIZE A WINDOW

1 Click the **Minimize** button (⬜).

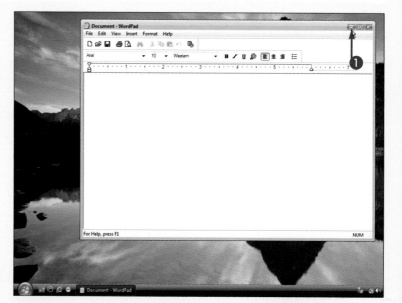

● The window disappears from the screen, but its taskbar button remains visible.

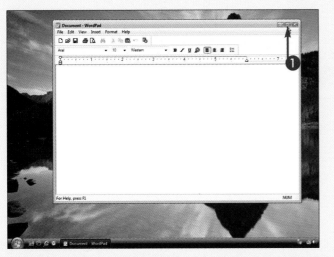

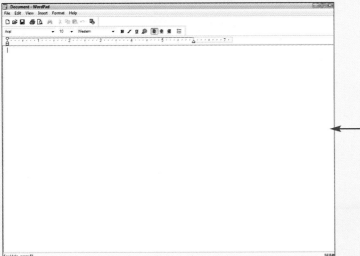

MAXIMIZE A WINDOW

1 Click the **Maximize** button ().

● The window enlarges to fill the entire desktop.

Note: *You can also maximize a window by double-clicking its title bar.*

Is there a faster way to minimize all my open windows?
The fastest way is to click the **Show desktop** icon (■) in the Quick Launch bar, just to the right of the **Start** button. You can also right-click the taskbar and then click **Show the Desktop**. This command minimizes all your open windows at once.

Is it possible to maximize a minimized window?
To do this, right-click the window's taskbar button, and then click **Maximize**.

continued

Work with Program Windows *(continued)*

For example, you should know how to *restore* a window. This means that you return the window to its original size and location after you have either minimized it or maximized it.

Are you ready for more window techniques? Windows Vista uses many windows, so the more you know, the faster and more efficiently you can work.

Work with Program Windows (continued)

RESTORE A WINDOW

1 If the window is maximized, click the **Restore** button (⧉).

If the window is minimized, click its taskbar button instead.

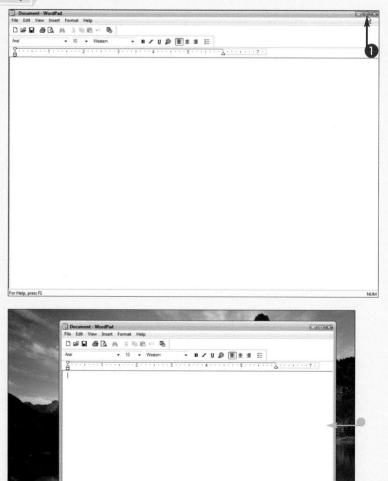

● The window returns to its previous size and location.

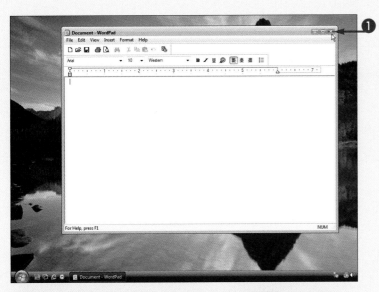

CLOSE A WINDOW

1 Click the **Close** button ().

The window disappears from the screen.

● If the window has a taskbar button, the button disappears from the taskbar.

Note: *If the window contains a document, the program may ask if you want to save any changes you made in the document before closing.*

Can I work with program windows via the keyboard?
Yes, you do this by using the *system menu* that comes with each window. Click the system menu icon in the upper-left corner to display the menu, press ⬆ and ⬇ on the keyboard to highlight the command you want, and then press Enter. If you choose **Move** or **Size** from the system menu, use the keyboard ⬆, ⬇, ⬅, and ➡ to move or size the window, and then press Enter.

continued

Work with Program Windows *(continued)*

If your windows overlap each other, making it hard to read what is in other windows, you can move the windows around or resize them.

Work with Program Windows *(continued)*

CHANGE THE WINDOW SIZE

1 Position the mouse ⌖ over the window border that you want to move.

● The ⌖ changes to a two-headed arrow (↕).

Note: *If the pointer does not change, it means the window cannot be resized.*

2 Click and drag the ↕ to make the window larger or smaller.

Windows Vista moves the border along with the ↕.

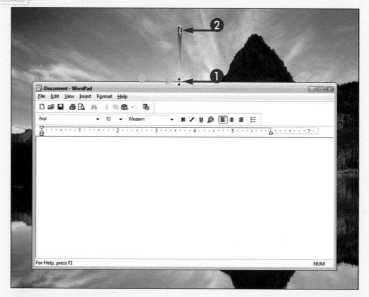

3 Release the mouse button.

● Windows Vista resizes the window.

Note: *To resize two borders at once, click and drag any corner of the window.*

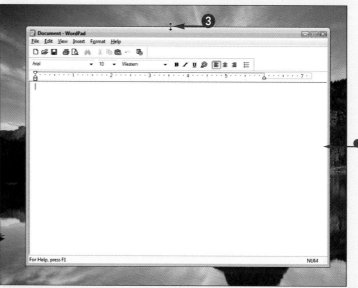

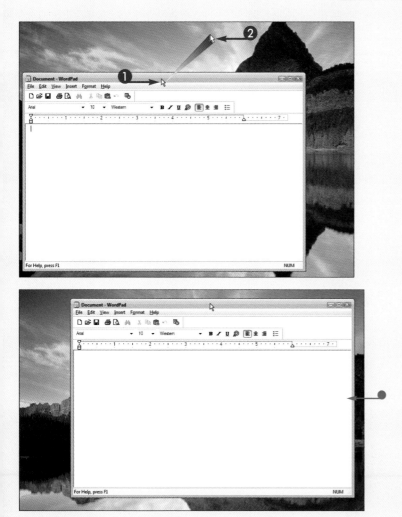

MOVE A WINDOW

1 Position the mouse ⌖ over an empty section of the window's title bar.

2 Click and drag the mouse ⌖ in the direction you want the window to move.

Windows Vista moves the window along with the mouse ⌖.

3 Release the mouse button.

● Windows Vista moves the window.

When I have several windows open, is there an easier way to size them so that none of the windows overlap?
Use Windows Vista's Side by Side feature: Right-click an empty section of the taskbar and then click **Show Windows Side by Side**. Windows Vista divides the desktop to give each window an equal amount of space.

When I have several windows open, is there an easier way to move them so that the windows are arranged neatly?
Use Windows Vista's Stack feature: Right-click an empty section of the taskbar and then click **Show Windows Stacked**. Windows Vista arranges the windows in a tidy diagonal pattern from the top-left corner of the desktop.

Using Scrollbars

If the entire content of a document does not fit inside a window, you can see the rest of the document by using the window's scrollbars to move vertically or horizontally.

Scrollbars also appear in many list boxes, so knowing how to work with scrollbars also helps you use dialog boxes.

SCROLL UP OR DOWN IN A WINDOW

1 Click the up arrow (▲) or down arrow (▼), or click and drag the vertical scroll box down or up to scroll through a window.

● The text scrolls down or up.

Trips v. Vacations - WordPad

File Edit View Insert Format Help

Times New Roman ▼ 12 ▼ Western ▼ **B** *I* U 🖉 ▤ ≡ ≡ ≣

There are *trips* and then there are *vacations*. On a trip you explore the new and the different; you welcome novelty, seek out the unusual, and turn left or right when your original intention had been to go straight. On a trip you *look*, wide-eyed (by which I mean more a mental state than a physical one) inwardly adjusting the aperture of your gaze to let in the maximum number of visual impressions. These are, in turn, the grist for some mulling mill, the end product of which is another chapter completed in the narrative that represents your life's remarkable (i.e., remark-able) events.

A vacation, on the other hand, has (or should have) a mindlessness that exists in a tranquil, ideally guiltless, contrast to the mindfulness of a trip. The proper vacation should represent the cessation of narration, a blissful thumbing-of-the-nose at time, schedules, events, and "experiences." The perfect (winter) vacation should consist of nothing more than entire days spent lazing on a warm, shady beach where the chief activities of reading well and watching the waves come in are punctuated only by the occasional meal, runs for drinks, and soothing dips in warm, enveloping waters.

The beach puts the brain in neutral by knocking out the higher reasoning centres as well as the lower-level action/stimulus nexus. The beach mechanisms—from the

For Help, press F1   NUM

Trips v. Vacations - WordPad

File Edit View Insert Format Help

Times New Roman ▼ 12 ▼ Western ▼ **B** *I* U 🖉 ▤ ≡ ≡ ≣

A vacation, on the other hand, has (or should have) a mindlessness that exists in a tranquil, ideally guiltless, contrast to the mindfulness of a trip. The proper vacation should represent the cessation of narration, a blissful thumbing-of-the-nose at time, schedules, events, and "experiences." The perfect (winter) vacation should consist of nothing more than entire days spent lazing on a warm, shady beach where the chief activities of reading well and watching the waves come in are punctuated only by the occasional meal, runs for drinks, and soothing dips in warm, enveloping waters.

The beach puts the brain in neutral by knocking out the higher reasoning centres as well as the lower-level action/stimulus nexus. The beach mechanisms—from the gentle, whispering breezes to the soft, walk-slowing sand, to the incessant waves that produce with each crash an equivalent series of alpha waves in the mind—create a kind of "call to inaction," an inner stillness that's the flip side, the lazy twin, of Zen enlightenment. It's a melancholic state that you could easily mistake for depression if it wasn't for the underlying feeling of well-being. It's a quicksandish lethargy where even the thought of energetic activity is not only laughable but also painful (a sort of mental pulled muscle).

For Help, press F1   NUM

SCROLL LEFT OR RIGHT IN A WINDOW

1 Click the left arrow (◄) or the right arrow (►), or click and drag the horizontal scroll box.

Trips v. Vacations - WordPad

File Edit View Insert Format Help

Times New Roman   12   Western   **B** *I* <u>U</u>

There are *trips* and then there are *vacations*. On a trip you explore different; you welcome novelty, seek out the unusual, and turn left original intention had been to go straight. On a trip you *look*, wide mean more a mental state than a physical one) inwardly adjusting gaze to let in the maximum number of visual impressions. These ar for some mulling mill, the end product of which is another chapter narrative that represents your life's remarkable (i.e., remark-able)

A vacation, on the other hand, has (or should have) a mindlessnes tranquil, ideally guiltless, contrast to the mindfulness of a trip. The should represent the cessation of narration, a blissful thumbing-of-schedules, events, and "experiences." The perfect (winter) vacatic nothing more than entire days spent lazing on a warm, shady beac activities of reading well and watching the waves come in are pun occasional meal, runs for drinks, and soothing dips in warm, enve

The beach puts the brain in neutral by knocking out the higher rea well as the lower-level action/stimulus nexus. The beach mechanis

For Help, press F1   NUM

---

* The text scrolls left or right.

Trips v. Vacations - WordPad

File Edit View Insert Format Help

Times New Roman   12   Western   **B** *I* <u>U</u>

then there are *vacations*. On a trip you explore the new and the me novelty, seek out the unusual, and turn left or right when your d been to go straight. On a trip you *look*, wide-eyed (by which I l state than a physical one) inwardly adjusting the aperture of your ximum number of visual impressions. These are, in turn, the grist l, the end product of which is another chapter completed in the ents your life's remarkable (i.e., remark-able) events.

ther hand, has (or should have) a mindlessness that exists in a less, contrast to the mindfulness of a trip. The proper vacation cessation of narration, a blissful thumbing-of-the-nose at time, nd "experiences." The perfect (winter) vacation should consist of ntire days spent lazing on a warm, shady beach where the chief well and watching the waves come in are punctuated only by the s for drinks, and soothing dips in warm, enveloping waters.

brain in neutral by knocking out the higher reasoning centres as vel action/stimulus nexus. The beach mechanisms—from the

For Help, press F1   NUM

SIMPLIFY IT

What is the wheel on my mouse used for?
Not everyone's mouse has a wheel, but if yours does, you can use the wheel for scrolling up or down in a document. It works the same way as clicking the up arrow (▲) or the down arrow (▼) does. Move the wheel backward, toward your arm, and the document scrolls down; move the wheel forward, toward your computer, and the document scrolls up.

Switch Between Programs

You can switch from one program to another using either the taskbar or the keyboard.

With Windows Vista, if you are *multitasking* — running two or more programs at once — you need to know how to switch from one to another.

Switch Between Programs

SWITCH PROGRAMS USING THE TASKBAR

① Click the taskbar button of the program to which you want to switch.

Note: *A program does not have to be minimized to the taskbar for you to use the program's taskbar button.*

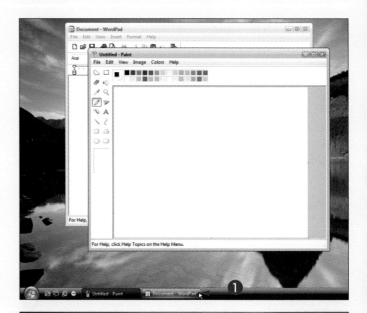

● Windows Vista brings the program's window to the foreground.

Note: *You can also switch to another window by clicking the window, even if it is the background.*

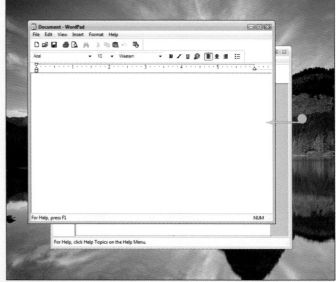

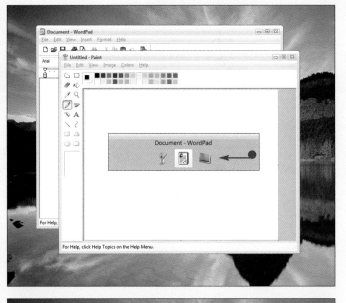

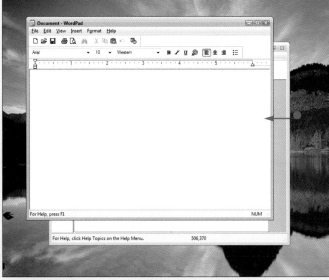

SWITCH PROGRAMS USING THE KEYBOARD

1 Hold down `Alt` and press `Tab`.

● Windows Vista displays thumbnail versions of the open windows and the desktop.

2 Press `Tab` until the window in which you want to work is selected.

3 Release `Alt`.

● Windows Vista brings the program's window to the foreground.

Can I see what is in a window before switching to it?
Yes. In fact, Windows Vista gives you three different ways to do this:

● Move the mouse ⬚ over a program's taskbar button. Windows Vista displays a thumbnail version of the program window.

● Hold down `Alt` and repeatedly press `Esc`. Each time you press `Esc`, Windows Vista brings a program window to the foreground. When you see the window you want, release `Alt`.

● On some systems, you can hold down ⊞ and repeatedly press `Tab`. Windows Vista displays the open windows as a 3-D stack, and each time you press `Tab`, Windows Vista brings a program window to the foreground. When you see the window you want, release ⊞.

Uninstall a Program

Removing unused programs frees up disk space and makes your All Programs menu easier to navigate.

When you plan to no longer use a program, you should uninstall it from your computer.

Uninstall a Program

1 Click **Start**.

2 Click **Control Panel**.

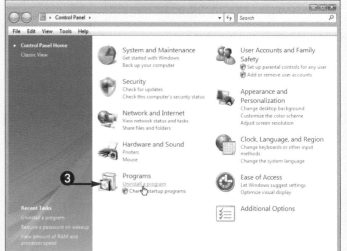

The Control Panel window appears.

3 Click **Uninstall a program**.

The Installed Programs window appears.

④ Click the program you want to uninstall.

⑤ Click **Uninstall** (or **Uninstall/ Change**).

● The program asks you to confirm that you want to uninstall it.

⑥ Click **Yes**.

The program's uninstall procedure begins.

⑦ Follow the instructions on the screen, which vary from program to program.

Is there a quicker way to uninstall a program?
Yes. Many programs come with their own uninstall command. Click **Start**, click **All Programs**, and then click the program name. If you see a command that includes the word **Uninstall**, click that command to begin the uninstall procedure.

What is the difference between an Automatic and a Custom uninstall?
Some programs give you a choice of uninstall procedures. The Automatic uninstall requires no input from you. It is the easiest, safest choice and therefore the one you should choose. The Custom uninstall gives you more control, but is more complex and only suitable for experienced users.

Chapter 3

Creating and Editing Documents

To get productive with Windows Vista, you need to know how to work with documents. In this chapter, you learn how to create, save, open, edit, and print documents.

Understanding Documents

Documents are files that you create or edit yourself. The four examples shown here are the basic document types that you can create using the programs that come with Windows Vista.

Text Document

A text document is one that includes only the characters that you see on your keyboard, plus a few others. A text document contains no special formatting, such as colored text or bold formatting, although you can change the font. In Windows Vista you normally use the Notepad program to create text documents (although you can also use WordPad).

Word Processing Document

A word processing document contains text and other symbols, but you can format those characters to improve the look of the document. For example, you can change the size, color, and typeface, and you can make words bold or italic. In Windows Vista, you use the WordPad program to create word processing — or Rich Text Format — documents.

Drawing

A drawing in this context is a digital image you create using special "tools" that create lines, boxes, polygons, special effects, and free-form shapes. In Windows Vista, you use the Paint program to create drawings.

E-Mail Message

An e-mail message is a document that you send to another person via the Internet. Most e-mail messages use plain text, but some programs support formatted text, images, and other effects. In Windows Vista, you use the Windows Mail program to create and send e-mail messages (see Chapter 11).

Create a Document

You can create a new document to hold your work.

Many Windows Vista programs (such as WordPad and Paint) create a new document for you automatically when you begin the program.

Create a Document

CREATE A DOCUMENT WITHIN A PROGRAM

1 Start the program with which you want to work.

2 Click **File**.

3 Click **New**.

Note: Another way to create a document is to click the **New Document** button (□).

Note: In most programs, you can also press `Ctrl` + `N` to create a new document.

● If the program supports more than one type of file, the program asks which type you want to create.

4 Click the document type you want.

5 Click **OK**.

The program creates the new document.

Save a Document

After you create a document and make any changes to it, you can save the document to preserve your work.

When you work on a document, Windows Vista stores the changes in your computer's memory, which is erased each time you shut down your computer. Saving the document preserves your changes on your computer's hard drive.

Save a Document

1 Click **File**.

2 Click **Save**.

Note: In most programs, you can also press **Ctrl** + **S** or click the **Save** button ().

Note: If you saved the document previously, your changes are now preserved. You do not need to follow the rest of the steps in this task.

If this is a new document that you have never saved before, the Save As dialog box appears.

3 Click here to see a list of your folders.

4 Click **Documents**.

Note: In most programs, the Documents folder is selected automatically when you save a document.

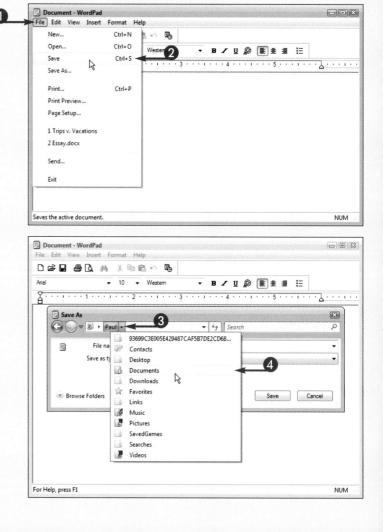

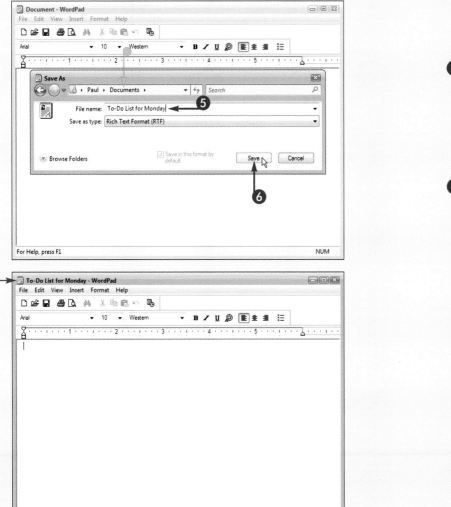

● Windows Vista opens the Documents folder.

5 Click in the **File name** text box and type the name you want to use for the document.

Note: *The name you type can be up to 255 characters long, but it cannot include the following characters: < > , ? : " \ **

6 Click **Save**.

● The file name you typed appears in the program's title bar.

Can I create different types of documents in a program?

Yes, in most programs. With WordPad, for example, you can create both word processing documents and text documents. However, a program such as Notepad only supports text documents. If the program supports multiple document types, the Save As dialog box includes a drop-down list named **Save as type** (or something similar). Use that list to choose the document type you want.

Open a Document

To work with a document that you have saved in the past, you need to open the document in the program that you used to create it.

Open a Document

 Start the program with which you want to work.

 Click **File**.

Note: If you see a list of the most recently opened documents near the bottom of the File menu, and you see the document you want, click the name to open it. You can skip the rest of the steps in this task.

❸ Click **Open**.

Note: In most programs, you can also press Ctrl *+* O *or click the **Open** button (📂).*

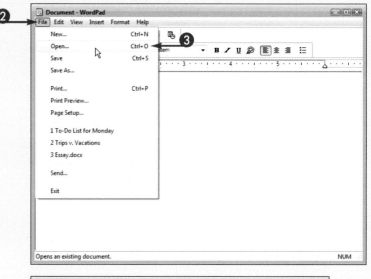

❹ Double-click **Documents**.

Note: In most programs, the Documents folder is selected automatically when you open a document.

Note: If you want to open the document from some other folder, click your user name in the Address bar and then double-click the folder.

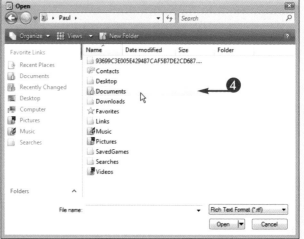

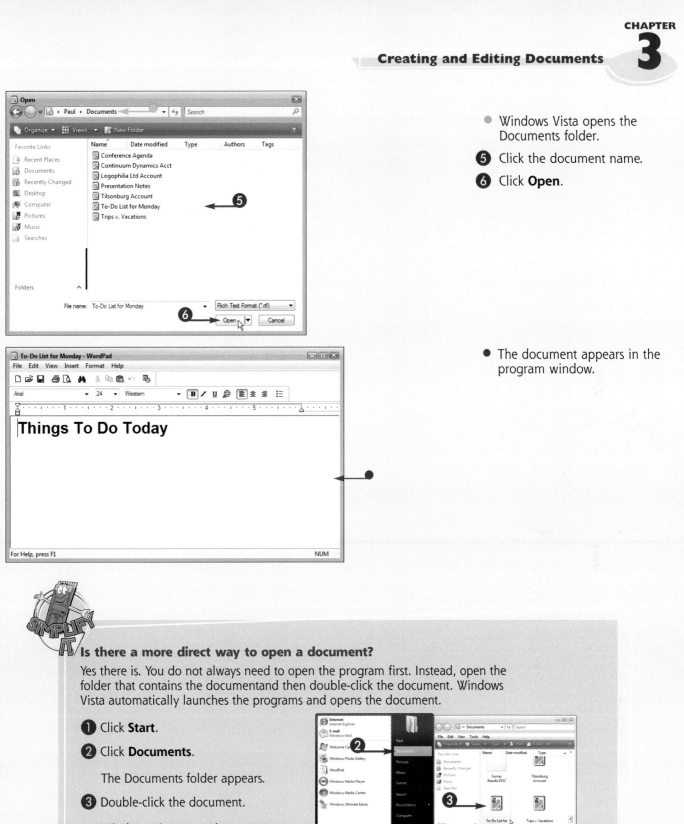

● Windows Vista opens the Documents folder.

⑤ Click the document name.

⑥ Click **Open**.

● The document appears in the program window.

Is there a more direct way to open a document?

Yes there is. You do not always need to open the program first. Instead, open the folder that contains the document and then double-click the document. Windows Vista automatically launches the programs and opens the document.

① Click **Start**.

② Click **Documents**.

The Documents folder appears.

③ Double-click the document.

Windows Vista starts the program in which you created the document and then opens the document.

49

Edit Document Text

When you work with a character-based file, such as a text or word processing document or an e-mail message, you need to know the basic techniques for editing, selecting, copying, and moving text.

Edit Document Text

DELETE CHARACTERS

① Click immediately to the left of the first character you want to delete.

● The cursor appears before the character.

② Press `Delete` until you have deleted all the characters you want.

Note: *An alternative method is to click immediately to the right of the last character you want to delete and then press `Backspace` until you have deleted all the characters you want.*

Note: *If you make a mistake, immediately click **Edit**, and then click **Undo**. Alternatively, press `Ctrl` + `Z` or click the **Undo** button (⟲).*

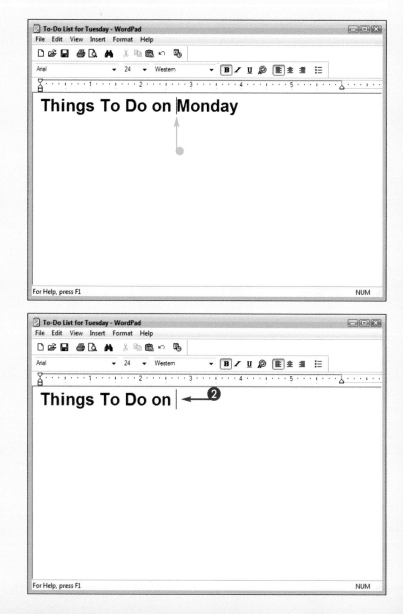

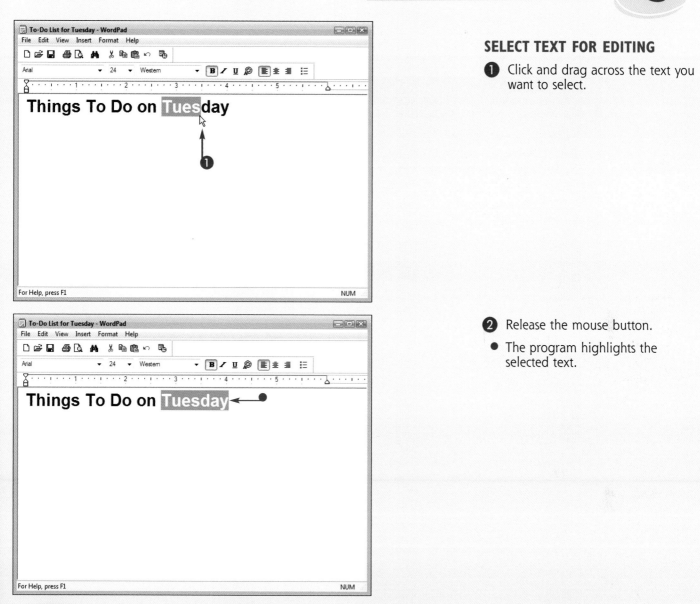

SELECT TEXT FOR EDITING

1 Click and drag across the text you want to select.

2 Release the mouse button.

- The program highlights the selected text.

Are there any shortcut methods I can use to select text in WordPad?
Yes. Here are the most useful ones:

- Click in the white space to the left of a line to select the line.
- Double-click a word to select it.
- Triple-click inside a paragraph to select it.
- Press **Ctrl** + **A** to select the entire document.
- For a long selection, click to the left of the first character you want to select, scroll to the end of the selection using the scroll bar, hold down **Shift**, and then click to the right of the last character you want to select.

continued

Edit Document
Text *(continued)*

Once you select some text, you can work with all of the selected characters together, which is much faster than working with one character at a time. You will find some examples in the rest of this task.

Edit Document Text *(continued)*

COPY TEXT

① Select the text you want to copy.

② Click **Edit**.

③ Click **Copy**.

Note: *In most programs, you can also press* Ctrl *+* C *or click the* **Copy** *button ().*

④ Click inside the document at the position where you want the copy of the text to appear.

The cursor appears in position you clicked.

⑤ Click **Edit**.

⑥ Click **Paste**.

Note: *In most programs, you can also press* Ctrl *+* V *or click the* **Paste** *button ().*

● The program inserts a copy of the selected text at the cursor position.

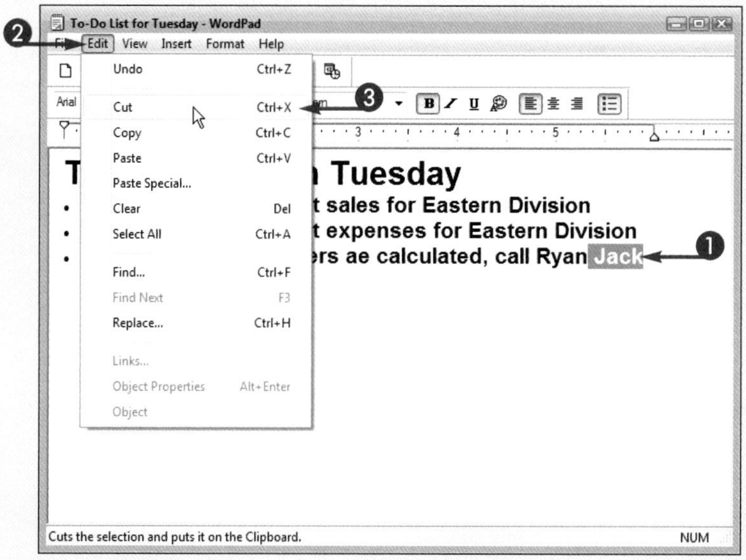

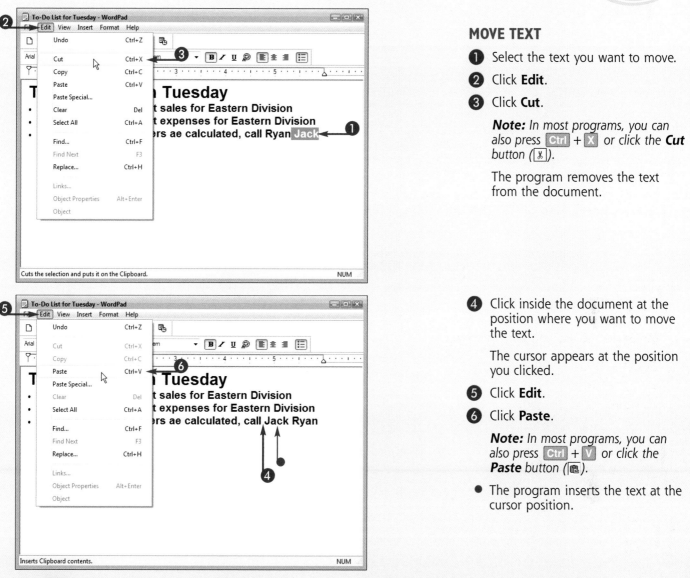

MOVE TEXT

1. Select the text you want to move.
2. Click **Edit**.
3. Click **Cut**.

   Note: *In most programs, you can also press* Ctrl *+* X *or click the* ***Cut*** *button* (✂).

   The program removes the text from the document.

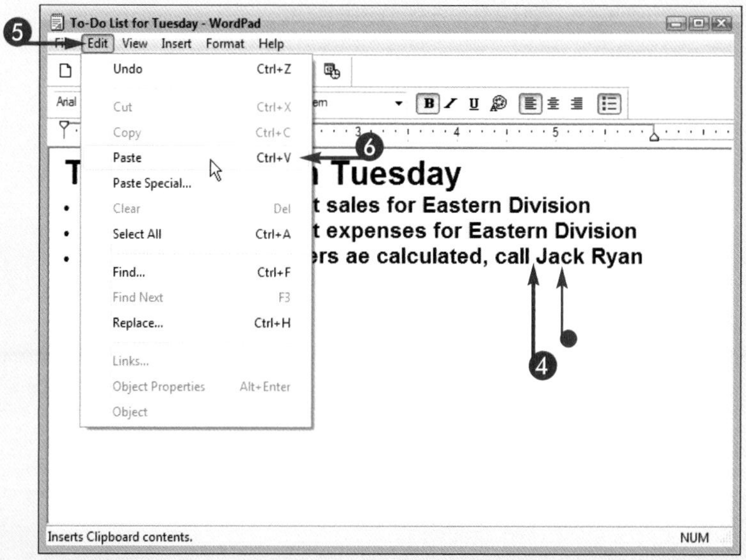

4. Click inside the document at the position where you want to move the text.

   The cursor appears at the position you clicked.

5. Click **Edit**.
6. Click **Paste**.

   Note: *In most programs, you can also press* Ctrl *+* V *or click the* ***Paste*** *button* (📋).

- The program inserts the text at the cursor position.

SIMPLIFY IT

How do I move and copy text with my mouse?

First, select the text with which you want to work. To move the selected text, place the mouse over the selection and then click and drag the text to the new position within the document.

To copy the selected text, place the mouse over the selection, hold down Ctrl, and then click and drag the text to the desired position within the document.

Change the Text Font

When you work in a word processing document, you can add visual appeal by changing the font formatting.

The font formatting includes attributes such as the typeface (the overall look of each character), style (bold or italic), size, or special effects (such as underline or colors).

Change the Text Font

① Select the text you want to format.

② Click **Format**.

③ Click **Font**.

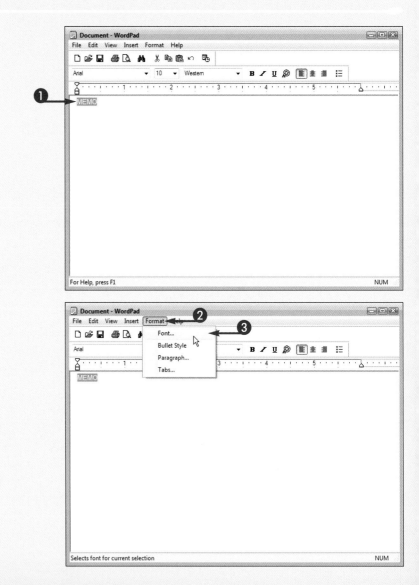

54

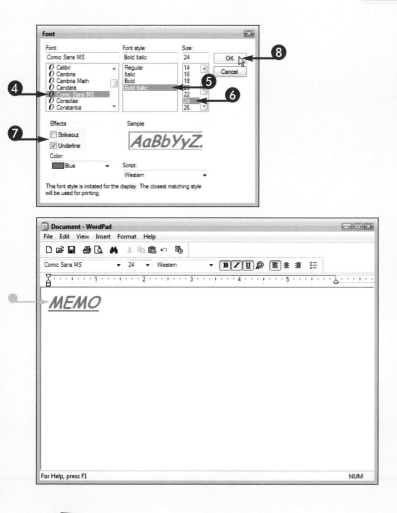

The Font dialog box appears.

Note: *The layout of the Font dialog box varies by program, but the one shown here is typical.*

④ In the Font list, click the typeface you want.

⑤ In the Font style list, click the style you want.

⑥ In the Size list, click the type size you want.

⑦ In the Effects group, click the controls to apply formatting (☐ changes to ☑).

⑧ Click **OK**.

● The program applies the font formatting to the selected text.

Note: *Here are some font shortcuts that work in most programs: For bold, press* Ctrl *+* B *or click the **Bold** button (* B *); for italics, press* Ctrl *+* I *or click the **Italic** button (* I *); for underline, press* Ctrl *+* U *or click the **Underline** button (* U *).*

How can I make the best use of fonts in my documents?

● Do not use many different typefaces in a single document. Stick to one, or at most two, typeface to avoid the "ransom note look."

● Avoid overly decorative typefaces because they are often difficult to read.

● Use bold only for document titles, subtitles, and headings.

● Use italics only to emphasize words and phrases, or for the titles of books and magazines.

● Use larger type sizes only for document titles, subtitles, and, possibly, the headings.

● If you change the text color, be sure to leave enough contrast between the text and the background. In general, dark text on a light background is the easiest to read.

Find Text

Most programs that work with text — including Windows Vista's WordPad and Notepad programs — have the Find feature.

> In large documents, when you need to find specific text, you can save a lot of time by using the program's Find feature, which searches the entire document in the blink of an eye.

Find Text

① Click **Edit**.

② Click **Find**.

> **Note:** In many programs, you can run the Find command by pressing `Ctrl` + `F`.

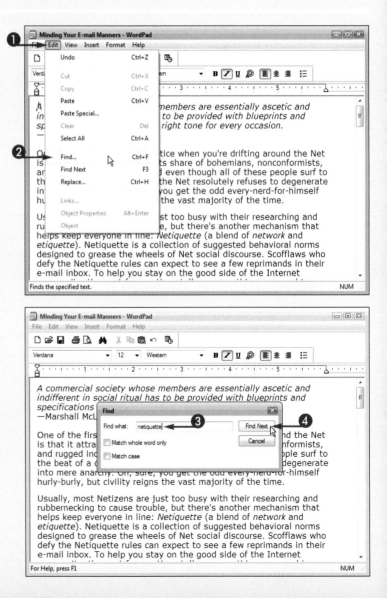

The Find dialog box appears.

③ Click in the **Find what** text box and type the text you want to find.

④ Click **Find Next**.

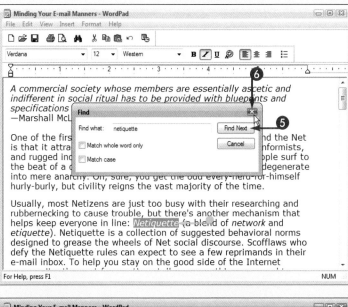

● The program selects the next instance of the search text.

Note: *If the search text does not exist in the document, the program displays a dialog box to let you know.*

⑤ If the selected instance is not the one you want, click **Find Next** until the program finds the correct instance.

⑥ Click the **Close** button (☒) to close the Find dialog box.

● The program leaves the found text selected.

When I search for a small word such as *the*, the program matches it in larger words such as *theme* and *bother*. How can I avoid this?
In the Find dialog box, click **Match whole word only** (☐ changes to ☑). This tells the program to match the search text only if it is a word on its own and not part of another word.

When I search for a name such as *Bill*, the program also matches the non-name *bill*. Is there a way to fix this?
In the Find dialog box, click **Match case** (☐ changes to ☑). This tells the program to match the search text only if it has the same mix of uppercase and lowercase letters that you specify in the **Find what** text box. If you type **Bill**, for example, the program matches only *Bill* and not *bill*.

Replace Text

Most programs that work with text — including Windows Vista's WordPad and Notepad programs — have the Replace feature.

Do you need to replace a word or part of a word with some other text? If you have several instances to replace, you can save time and do a more accurate job if you let the program's Replace feature replace the word for you.

Replace Text

1. Click **Edit**.

2. Click **Replace**.

   Note: In many programs, you can run the Replace command by pressing `Ctrl` + `H`.

The Replace dialog box appears.

3. In the **Find what** text box, enter the text you want to find.

4. Click in the **Replace with** text box and type the text you want to use as the replacement.

5. Click **Find Next**.

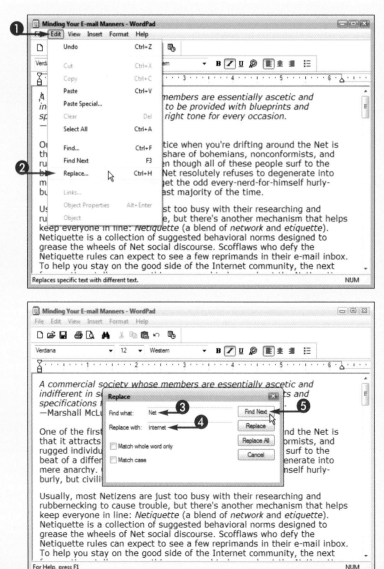

● The program selects the next instance of the search text.

Note: If the search text does not exist in the document, the program displays a dialog box to let you know.

⑥ If the selected instance is not the one you want, click **Find Next** until the program finds the correct instance.

⑦ Click **Replace**.

● The program replaces the selected text with the replacement text.

● The program selects the next instance of the search text.

⑧ Repeat Steps **6** and **7** until you have replaced all of the instances you want to replace.

⑨ Click the **Close** button (☒) to close the Replace dialog box.

SIMPLIFY IT

Is there a faster way to replace every instance of the search text with the replacement text?
Yes. In the Replace dialog box, click **Replace All**. This tells the program to replace every instance of the search text with the replacement text. However, you should exercise some caution with this feature because it may make some replacements that you did not intend. Click **Find Next** a few times to make sure the matches are correct. Also, consider clicking the **Match whole word only** and **Match case** check boxes (☐ changes to ☑), as described in the "Find Text" task in this chapter.

Print a Document

When you need a hard copy of your document, either for your files or to distribute to someone else, you can get a hard copy by sending the document to your printer.

Print a Document

1 Turn on your printer.

2 Open the document you want to print.

3 Click **File**.

4 Click **Print**.

Note: In many programs, you can select the Print command by pressing **Ctrl** + **P** or by clicking the **Print** button (🖨).

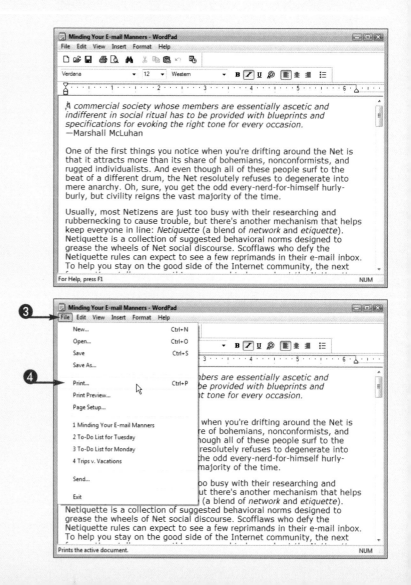

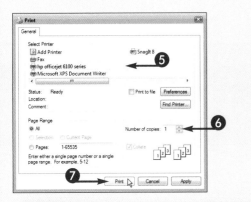
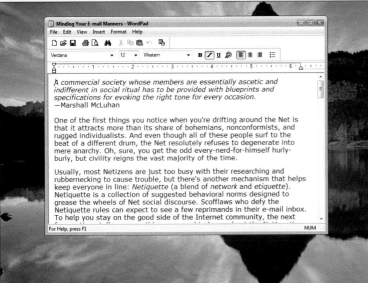

The Print dialog box appears.

Note: The layout of the Print dialog box varies from program to program. The WordPad version shown here is a typical example.

⑤ If you have more than one printer, click the printer you want to use.

⑥ Use the **Number of copies** 🔢 to specify the number of copies to print.

⑦ Click **Print**.

● Windows Vista prints the document. The print icon (🖨) appears in the taskbar's notification area while the document prints.

How do I print only part of a document?
Most programs enable you to use the following methods to print only part of the document:

● Print selected text: Select the text you want to print. In the Print dialog box, click **Selection** (⚪ changes to ⚫).

● Print a specific page: Place the cursor on the page you want to print. In the Print dialog box, click **Current Page** (⚪ changes to ⚫).

● Print a range of pages: In the Print dialog box, click **Pages** (⚪ changes to ⚫). In the text box, type the first page number, a dash (–), and the last page number (for example, 1–5).

Chapter 4

Working with Images

Whether you load your images from a digital camera or a scanner, download them from the Internet, or draw them yourself, Windows Vista comes with a number of useful tools for working with those images.

Open the Pictures Folder

Before you can work with your images, you need to view them on your computer. You do that by opening Windows Vista's Pictures folder, which is a special folder designed specifically for storing images.

Open the Pictures Folder

① Click **Start**.

② Click **Pictures**.

The Pictures folder appears.

Preview
an Image

You can preview any
saved image file using the
Preview pane in the Pictures folder.
The Preview pane, located at the
bottom of the window, also displays
details about the file, such as the
file type, dimensions,
and size.

You can also use the
Preview pane to
preview images stored
in *subfolders* —
folders stored within
the main Pictures
folder.

Preview an Image

1 Click the image file you want to
preview.

● The Preview pane area of the
folder window shows a preview of
the image.

● Details about the image file appear
here.

View Your Images

If you want to look at several images, you can use Windows Vista's Photo Gallery Viewer to navigate backwards and forwards through the images in the Pictures folder.

You can also use the Photo Gallery Viewer to zoom in and out of an image and to run an image slide show.

View Your Images

① Click the image you want to view first.

② Click the **Preview** ▐.

③ Click **Windows Photo Gallery**.

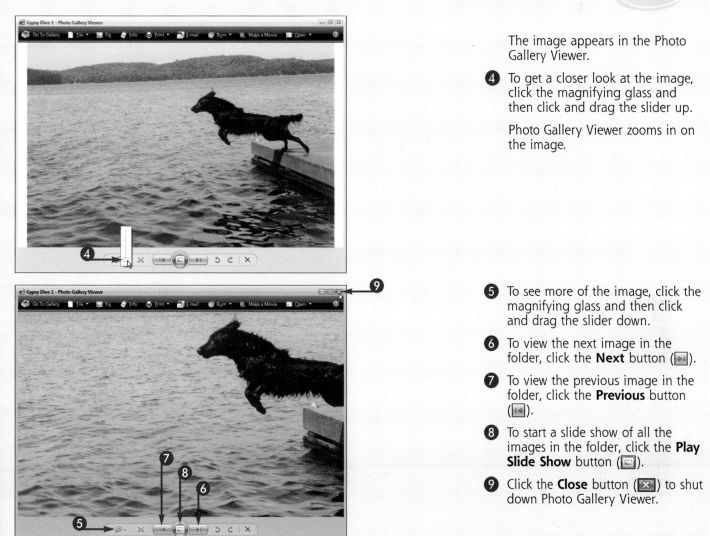

The image appears in the Photo Gallery Viewer.

④ To get a closer look at the image, click the magnifying glass and then click and drag the slider up.

Photo Gallery Viewer zooms in on the image.

⑤ To see more of the image, click the magnifying glass and then click and drag the slider down.

⑥ To view the next image in the folder, click the **Next** button (▶).

⑦ To view the previous image in the folder, click the **Previous** button (◀).

⑧ To start a slide show of all the images in the folder, click the **Play Slide Show** button (▣).

⑨ Click the **Close** button (✕) to shut down Photo Gallery Viewer.

Is there a way I can view my pictures without using the Photo Gallery Viewer?

Yes, you can change the Picture folder's view to display large thumbnails – scaled-down versions of the actual images:

① Click the **Views** ▾.

② Click **Extra Large Icons**.

● Windows Vista displays the images as thumbnails.

Scan an Image

You can create a digital copy of a photo or other image by using a document scanner. The scanner copies the image and stores it as a file on your computer.

For example, you can scan a photo to e-mail to friends or publish on a Web page. You can also scan a logo or other image to use in a document.

Scan an Image

① Turn on your scanner and position a photo on the scanner bed.

② Click **Start**.

③ Click **All Programs**.

④ Click **Windows Photo Gallery**.

The Windows Photo Gallery appears.

⑤ Click **File**.

⑥ Click **Import from Camera or Scanner**.

The Import Pictures and Videos dialog box appears.

⑦ Click the scanner you want to use.

⑧ Click **Import**.

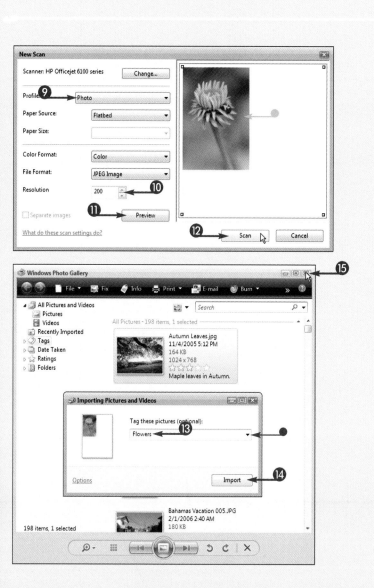

The New Scan dialog box appears.

⑨ Click the **Profile** ⬝ and then click **Photo**.

⑩ Click the **Resolution** ⬍ to specify the resolution of the scan.

Note: The higher the resolution, the sharper the image, but the larger the resulting file.

⑪ Click **Preview**.

● A preview of the scanned image appears here.

⑫ Click **Scan**.

Windows Vista scans the image.

The Importing Pictures and Videos dialog box appears.

⑬ Type a word or phrase that describes the photo.

● If you have typed text in this dialog box before, you can reuse the text by clicking ⬝ and then clicking the text.

⑭ Click **Import**.

The Windows Photo Gallery imports the image to your computer.

⑮ Click the **Close** button (⬚) to shut down Windows Photo Gallery.

How do I view a picture I have previously scanned?
Windows Photo Gallery stores the image in the Pictures folder. It creates a new folder, the name of which is the current date followed by whatever word or phrase you type in the Importing Pictures and Videos dialog box; for example, 2006-08-23, Flower. Open the subfolder to see your scanned picture. You can also click Recently Imported in Windows Photo Gallery to see images you have recently scanned.

My scanner does not appear in the Import Pictures and Videos dialog box. Why not?
Make sure your scanner is connected properly to your computer and is turned on. You may need to insert the CD that comes with the scanner to install the device correctly. If it still does not work, your scanner probably comes with its own software program on the CD. You can use that program to operate the scanner.

Import Images from a Digital Camera

Once you have the digital photos on your system, you can view, make repairs to, or print the images.

You can import photos from a digital camera and save them on your computer. If your camera stores the photos on a memory card, you can also attach a memory card reader to your computer and upload the digital photos from the removable drive that Windows Vista sets up.

Import Images from a Digital Camera

① Plug in your camera or memory storage card reader.

Note: *If you see the AutoPlay dialog box, click* **Import pictures using Windows** *and go to Step* **9**.

② Click **Start**.

③ Click **All Programs**.

④ Click **Windows Photo Gallery**.

The Windows Photo Gallery appears.

⑤ Click **File**.

⑥ Click **Import from Camera or Scanner**.

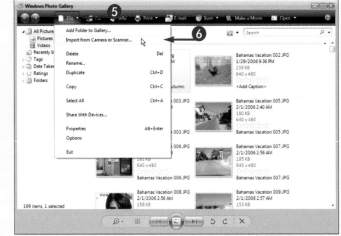

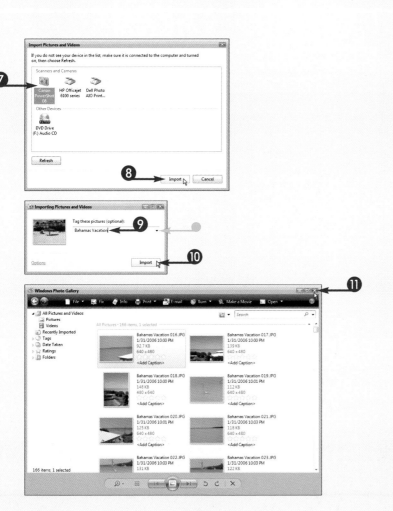

The Import Pictures and Videos dialog box appears.

⑦ Click the camera or removable drive you want to use.

⑧ Click **Import**.

The Importing Pictures and Videos dialog box appears.

⑨ Type a word or phrase that describes the photos.

● If you have typed text in this dialog box before, you can reuse the text by clicking ⬝ and then clicking the text.

⑩ Click **Import**.

Windows Vista begins importing the digital photos.

The Windows Photo Gallery appears and displays the recently imported items, which include your scanned image.

Note: If your digital camera includes video clips, those clips are also imported to Windows Photo Gallery.

⑪ Click the **Close** button (⊠) to shut down Windows Photo Gallery.

How do I view the imported photos?
Windows Vista stores the imported digital photos in the Pictures folder. It creates a new subfolder, the name of which is the current date followed by whatever word or phrase you type in the Importing Pictures and Videos dialog box. For example, if the current date is August 23, 2006 and you typed **Bahamas Vacation** in the text box, the new subfolder will be named 2006-08-23, Bahamas Vacation. Open the subfolder to see your imported digital photos.

Repair a Digital Image

The Fix window enables you to adjust an image's brightness, contrast, color temperature, tint, and saturation. You can also crop and rotate an image and fix red eye.

You can use Windows Vista's new Photo Gallery to improve the look of digital photos and other images. The Photo Gallery includes a special Fix window that offers a number of tools for repairing various image attributes.

Repair a Digital Image

① Click **Start**.

② Click **All Programs**.

③ Click **Windows Photo Gallery**.

Windows Photo Gallery appears.

④ Click the image you want to repair.

⑤ Click **Fix**.

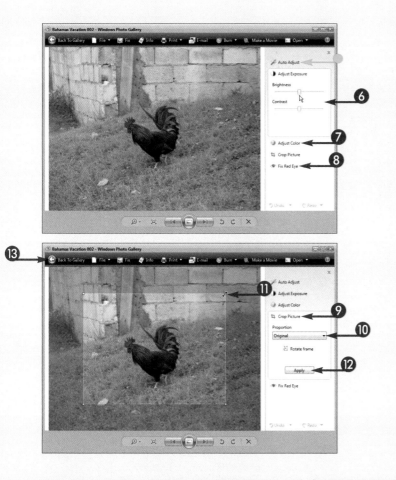

The Fix window appears.

6 To change the exposure, click **Adjust Exposure** and then click and drag the **Brightness** and **Contrast** sliders.

7 To change the color, click **Adjust Color** and then click and drag the **Color Temperature**, **Tint**, and **Saturation** sliders.

● If you are not sure how to use these tools, click **Auto Adjust** to have Photo Gallery make the adjustments for you.

8 To remove red eye from a photo, click **Fix Red Eye**.

9 To crop the picture, first click **Crop Picture**.

10 Click the **Proportion** and choose the dimensions you want.

*Note: Click **Original** to keep the same relative height and width; click **Custom** to crop to any height and width.*

11 Click and drag the handles to set the new size of the image.

12 Click **Apply**.

13 When you are done, click **Back To Gallery**.

Photo Gallery applies the repairs.

How did my photo end up sideways?
When you take a vertical shot with your digital camera, your photo appears sideways when you download the image to your computer. You may also have scanned the image vertically instead of horizontally. In the Fix window, click ⟲ to rotate the image counterclockwise; click ⟳ to rotate the image clockwise.

I do not like the repairs I made to my image. Can I get the original image back?
Yes, you can. The Photo Gallery always keeps a backup copy of the original image, just in case. To undo all your changes and get the original image back, click the image and then click **Fix**. In the Fix window, click **Revert** and then click **Revert to Original** (or press **Ctrl** + **R**).

Print an Image

You can print a single image or multiple images. If you work with multiple images, you can print them individually or print two or more images per sheet.

You can print an image from the Pictures folder, or from any subfolder in the Pictures folder. When you activate the Print task, the Print Pictures dialog box appears. You can use this dialog box to choose a printer and a layout, and to send the image to the printer.

Print an Image

① In the Pictures folder, select the image or images you want to print.

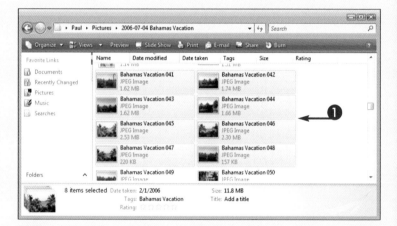

② Click **Print**.

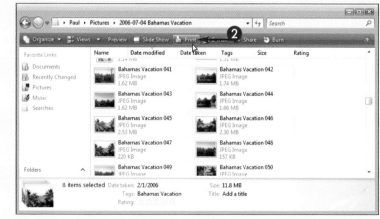

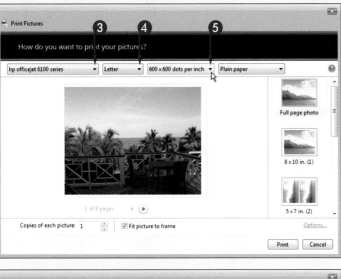

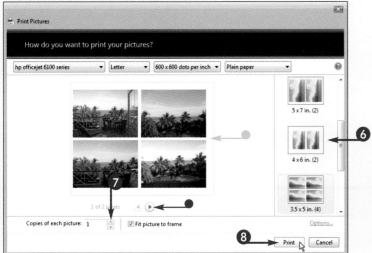

The Print Pictures dialog box appears.

③ If you use more than one printer with your computer, click ⊡ and click the printer you want to use.

④ Click ⊡ and click the type of paper you are using.

⑤ Click ⊡ and click printout quality you prefer.

Note: Print quality is measured in dots per inch (dpi). The higher the dpi value, the better the print quality.

⑥ Click the layout you want to use for the printed image.

● The wizard displays a preview of the printout.

● Click the **Next** button (▶) to see previews of other pages.

⑦ Click ⬍ to select the number of copies you want.

⑧ Click **Print**.

The wizard sends your image or images to the printer.

What type of paper should I use for my photo printouts?
Depending on the type of printer you are using, you can find a variety of photo-quality paper types for printing out your digital photographs. Photo-quality paper, though more expensive than multipurpose paper, is designed to create a more permanent image and improve the resolution and color of the printed images. Photo-quality paper comes in glossy and matte finishes, as well as variations of each. Be sure to select a photo-quality paper that your printer manufacturer recommends.

Chapter 5

Playing Music and Other Media

Using Windows Media Player, you can listen to audio files and music CDs, watch video files, play DVDs, and even create your own music CDs. Using Windows Media Center, you can view pictures and videos on your TV, and listen to audio files through your stereo.

Open and Close Windows Media Player

Windows Vista includes Windows Media Player to enable you to play back and record audio as well as view video. To begin using the program, you must first learn how to find and open the Windows Media Player window. When you finish using the program, you can close the Windows Media Player window to free up computer processing power.

Open and Close Windows Media Player

① Click **Start**.

② Click **All Programs**.

③ Click **Windows Media Player**.

● After you have used Windows Media Player once, you can also click the Windows Media Player icon in the Quick Launch toolbar.

● The Windows Media Player window appears, displaying the **Library** tab.

④ When you have finished with Media Player, click the **Close** button (⊠) to close the window.

The Windows Media Player window closes.

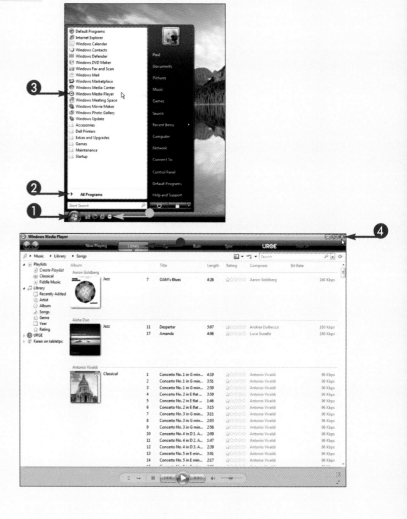

Navigate the Media Player Window

Familiarizing yourself with the various elements of the Windows Media Player window is a good idea so that you can easily navigate and activate elements when you are ready to play audio files or view videos and DVDs.

Title Bar
The title bar displays the name of the program.

Tabs
The tabs are links to the key features of Windows Media Player.

List Pane
The playlist pane displays the individual tracks on a CD or DVD, or any song names in a customized playlist.

Media Information
This pane displays a subset of information about the current content, such as the album art and title and the length of the song or video.

Playback Controls
These buttons control how a video or music file plays, and enable you to make adjustments to the sound.

Video/Visualization Pane
This pane displays the current video. For audio, it displays visualizations or the album cover art.

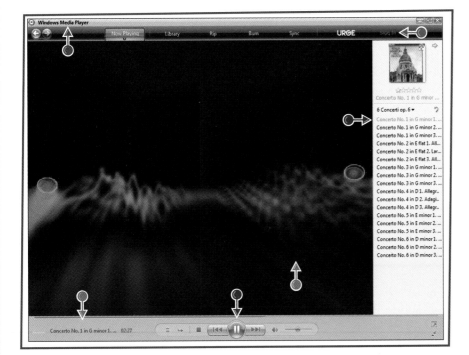

Using the Library

When you first start using Windows Media Player, you should add the media files on your computer to the Library.

You can use the Library feature in Windows Media Player to manage all of the media files on your computer, including audio files that you listen to with Windows Media Player. The Library also enables you to organize links to other digital content, such as music on the Internet.

ADD MEDIA FILES TO THE LIBRARY

1 Click the **Library** tab.

2 Click the **Library** ⏷.

● Windows Media Player displays a list of Library options.

3 Click **Add to Library**.

The Add to Library dialog box appears.

4 Click **My personal folders** (◎ changes to ◉).

5 Click **OK**.

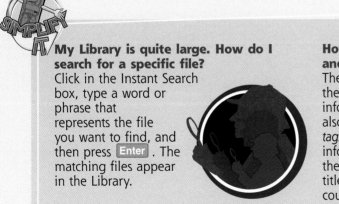

A dialog box appears, displaying the progress of the search.

⑥ When the search is complete, click **Close**.

VIEW FILES IN THE LIBRARY

● The Navigation pane displays folders that provide different views of the files in the Library.

① Click the folder you want to use.

② If the folder displays subfolders, double-click a subfolder to see its files.

● You can use the Instant Search box to search for music.

My Library is quite large. How do I search for a specific file?
Click in the Instant Search box, type a word or phrase that represents the file you want to find, and then press Enter. The matching files appear in the Library.

How does the Library create its folders and subfolders?
The Library automatically groups music into the categories based on their media content information. Media content information, also called *metadata* or *tags*, includes information such as the artist name, song title, rating, play count, and composer. Media content information also identifies the file type.

Play an Audio or a Video File

Windows Media Player uses the Library to play audio files that you store on your computer. When you select an audio file from a Library folder and play it in Windows Media Player, you can also switch to the Now Playing tab to view a visualization along with the song.

Play an Audio or a Video File

① Click the **Library** tab.

② Open the folder containing the audio or video file that you want to play.

③ Click the audio or video file name.

Note: See the "Using the Library" task to learn more about working with the Library's folder.

④ Click the **Play** button (▶).

Windows Media Player begins playing the audio or video file.

● You can click the **Now Playing** tab to view a visualization or album art while the audio file plays.

● You can use playback buttons, such as the **Stop** button (■), to control how the song or video plays.

Note: See the "Play a Music CD" task to learn more about the playback buttons.

Adjust the Volume

You can adjust the volume in Windows Media Player up or down to get the audio just right.

Adjust the Volume

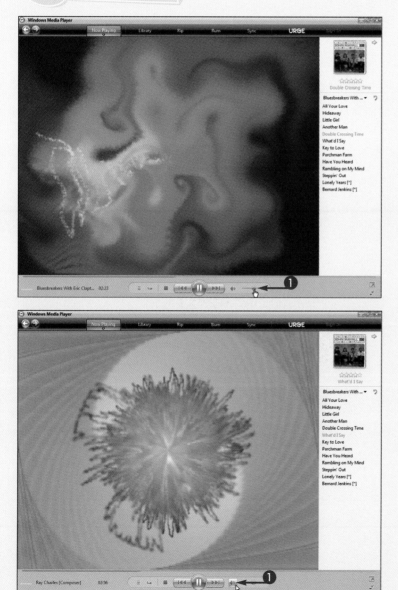

TURN VOLUME UP OR DOWN

① Click and drag the **Volume** slider left (to reduce the volume) or right (to increase the volume).

MUTE THE VOLUME

① Click the **Mute** button (▣).

Note: To restore the volume, click the **Sound** button (▣).

Play a Music CD

You can play your favorite music CDs in Windows Media Player. The Now Playing page displays the individual tracks on the CD in the List pane, and the Now Video/Visualization pane pulsates with the musical beats as the CD plays.

Play a Music CD

PLAY A CD

① Insert a music CD into your computer's CD or DVD drive.

The AutoPlay dialog box appears.

② Click **Play audio CD using Windows Media Player**.

The Windows Media Player window appears and begins playing the first song.

● This area displays the current visualization or album art.

● The playlist displays each song on the CD, along with the song length.

● On commercial CDs, the album cover appears here.

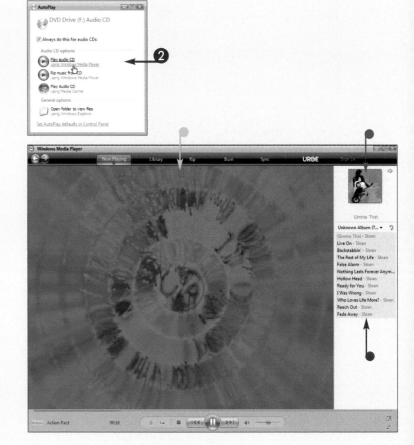

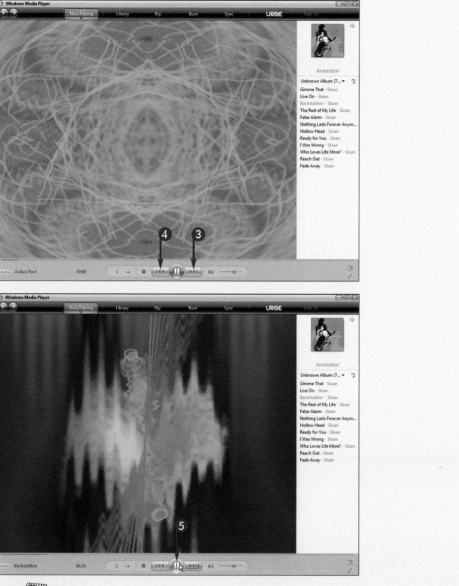

SKIP A TRACK

3 Click the **Next** button (▶▶|) to skip to the next track.

4 Click the **Previous** button (|◀◀) to skip to the previous track.

PAUSE AND RESUME PLAY

5 Click the **Pause** button (||).

Windows Media Player pauses playback.

6 Click the **Play** button (▶).

Windows Media Player resumes playback where you left off.

Can I change the CD's audio levels?
Yes. Windows Media Player has a graphic equalizer component with which you can work. To display it, click the **Now Playing** tab ⊡, click **Enhancements**, and then click **Graphic Equalizer**. Use the sliders to set the audio levels. You can click the **Next Enhancement** button (▣) to see other enhancements.

Can I change visualizations during playback?
Yes. You can click the **Now Playing** tab ⊡ and then click **Visualizations** to see a list of visualization categories. Click a category and then click the visualization you want to view. The visualizations in the Battery category are fun to play with, as their names suggest: **dance of the freaky circles**, **green is not your enemy**, **spider's last moment**, and **my tornado is resting**.

continued

Play a Music CD

(continued)

You can use the playback buttons at the bottom of the Windows Media Player window to control how a CD plays. For example, you can stop a CD and then select another song to play, or you can pause play if you have to leave the computer.

Play a Music CD *(continued)*

STOP PLAY

⑦ Click the **Stop** button (■).

Windows Media Player stops playback.

If you click the **Play** button (▶) after clicking the **Stop** button (■), the current song starts over again.

PLAY ANOTHER SONG

⑧ In the Playlist pane, double-click the song you want to play.

Windows Media Player begins playing the song.

● The current song title appears here.

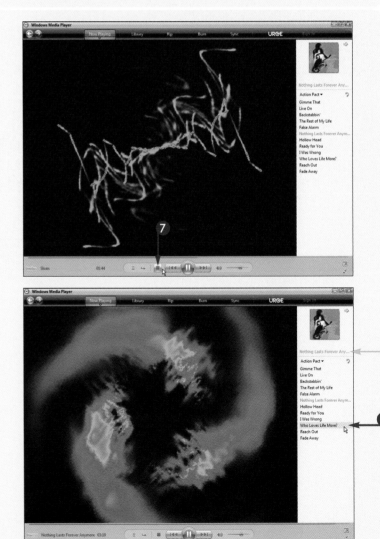

REPEAT THE CD

⑨ Click the **Turn Repeat On** button (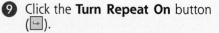).

Windows Media Player restarts the CD after the last track finishes playing.

PLAY SONGS RANDOMLY

⑩ Click the **Turn Shuffle On** button (▤).

Windows Media Player shuffles the order of play.

My Playlist pane does not list the song titles. Why not?

When you play a music CD, Windows Media Player tries to gather information about the album encoded in the CD. However, if it cannot ascertain song titles, then it displays track numbers instead. To type a song title, click the **Library** tab, click **Now Playing**, right-click the track, and click **Edit** from the menu that appears. Windows Media Player highlights the song in the playlist. Type a song title and press **Enter**. You can also press **F2** to edit a song title.

Can I change the order in which the CD's songs play?

Yes. You can shuffle the playlist to create a random order of songs. Click the **Now Playing** tab to display the visualization and the playlist on the right. Click ▾ beside the album title and then click **Shuffle List Now** in the menu that appears. Windows Media Player randomizes the playlist.

Copy Tracks from a Music CD

The Library helps you to organize and manage audio files on your computer. After you add a music track, you can play it from the Library tab.

You can add tracks from a music CD to the Library in Windows Media Player. This enables you to listen to an album without having to put the CD into your CD or DVD drive each time. The process of adding tracks from a CD is called *copying*, or *ripping*, in Windows Vista.

Copy Tracks from a Music CD

① Insert a CD into your computer's CD or DVD drive.

② Click the **Rip** tab.

③ If you have multiple disc drives, click the drive containing the music CD.

Windows Media Player displays a list of the CD's tracks.

④ Click the CD tracks that you do not want to copy (☑ changes to ☐).

⑤ Click **Start Rip**.

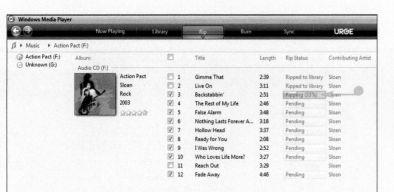

Windows Media Player begins
copying the track or tracks.

● The Rip Status column displays the
copy progress.

● After each file is copied, the Rip
Status column displays a Ripped to
library message.

● The copy is complete when all the
tracks you selected display the
Ripped to library status.

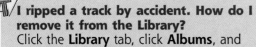

**I ripped a track by accident. How do I
remove it from the Library?**
Click the **Library** tab, click **Albums**, and
then double-click the album that you ripped
to display a list of the
tracks. Right-click the
track that you want
to remove, and then
click **Delete** from the
menu that appears.
When Windows Vista
asks you to confirm the
deletion, click **Yes**.

Can I adjust the quality of the copies?
Yes. You do that by changing the *bit rate*,
which is a measure of how much of the CD's
original data gets copied to your computer.
This is measured in kilobits per second
(Kbps): The higher the
value, the higher the
quality, but the more
disk space each track
takes up. Click the
Rip ⏷, click **Bit Rate**
from the menu that
appears, and then click
the value you want.

Create a Playlist

A *playlist* is a collection of songs, or music tracks you copy from a music CD, store on your computer hard drive, or download from the Internet. You can create customized playlists in Windows Media Player that play only the songs that you want to hear.

Create a Playlist

1. Click the **Library** tab.
2. Double-click **Playlists**.
3. Click **Create Playlist**.

- Windows Media Player creates a new playlist folder.
4. Type a name for the new playlist.
5. Press **Enter**.

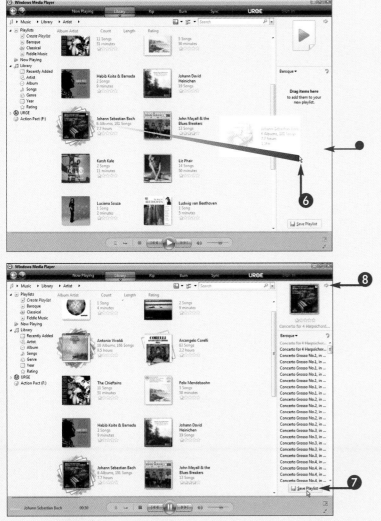

● The List pane appears.

⑥ Click and drag items from the Library and drop them inside the List pane.

⑦ Click **Save Playlist**.

⑧ Click the **Hide list pane** arrow (⬜) to close the List pane.

Can I add items to an existing playlist?
Yes. Click the **Library** tab and then locate the item you want to add. Right-click the item, click **Add to**, and then click the name of the playlist.

How can I rearrange my playlist songs in random order?
Right-click your playlist and then click **Edit in List Pane** to open the playlist and List pane. Click ⬝ beside the playlist name and then click **Shuffle List Now**.

Burn Music
Files to a CD

You can copy, or *burn*, music files from your computer onto a CD. Burning CDs is a great way to create customized CDs that you can listen to on the computer or in a portable device. You can burn music files from within the Windows Media Player window.

Burn Music Files to a CD

① Insert a blank CD into your computer's recordable CD drive.

② Click the **Burn** tab.

● The Burn List appears.

③ Click and drag items from the Library and drop them inside the Burn List.

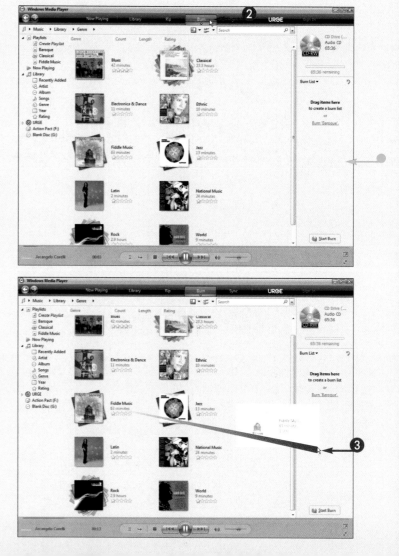

- Windows Media Player adds the files to the Burn List.

- Windows Media Player updates the approximate time remaining on the disc.

④ Repeat Step **3** to add more files to the Burn List.

⑤ Click **Start Burn**.

Windows Media Player converts the files to CD tracks and copies them to the CD.

- The Burn tab shows the progress of the burn.

  Note: *When the recording is complete, Windows Media Player automatically ejects the disc. Do not attempt to eject the disc yourself before the burn is finished.*

What is the difference between CD-R and CD-RW discs?

CD-R stands for *CD-Recordable*, and it enables you to record data to the disc but not erase or overwrite it. That is, after you finalize a CD-R disc, you cannot add more data to the disc later. CD-RW stands for *CD-ReWritable*, and it enables you to record data to the disc as often as you need.

What happens if I have more music than can fit on a single disc?

You can still add all the music you want to burn to the Burn List. Windows Media Player fills the first disc and then starts on a second disk (look for Next Disc in the Burn List). After the program finishes burning the first disc, it prompts you to insert the next one.

Play a DVD

Depending on how you set up your DVD drive and Windows Media Player, your DVD may begin playing as soon as you insert it. If it does not, you can follow the steps in this task to initiate playback.

You can use Windows Media Player to play DVDs. Windows Media Player enables you to watch any multimedia items stored on a DVD, such as movies and video footage.

Play a DVD

① Insert a DVD into your computer's DVD drive.

Note: *If you see the AutoPlay dialog box, click* **Play DVD Video using Windows Media Player** *and then skip to Step* **6**.

② Launch Windows Media Player.

③ Click the **Library** tab.

④ Right-click the DVD.

⑤ Click **Play**.

● Windows Media Player plays the DVD and displays the built-in menu.

● The tracks appear in the Playlist pane.

DVD menu items can vary in appearance and use different layouts.

⑥ Click the menu item or feature you want to play.

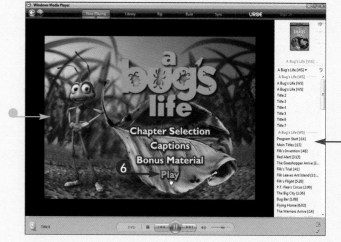

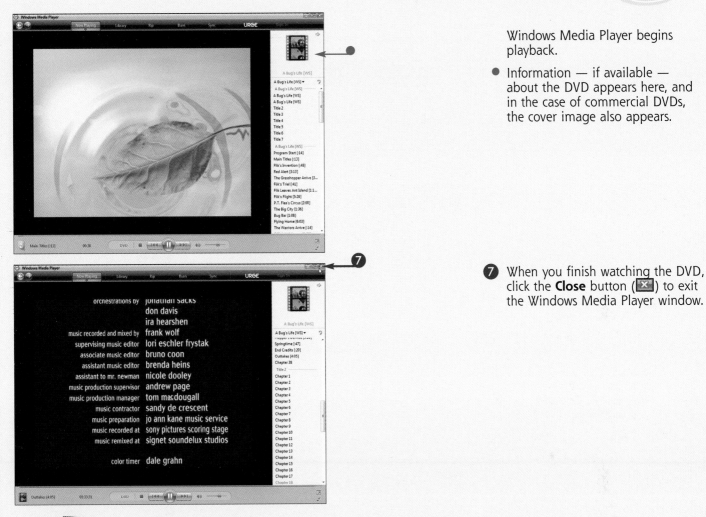

Windows Media Player begins playback.

● Information — if available — about the DVD appears here, and in the case of commercial DVDs, the cover image also appears.

⑦ When you finish watching the DVD, click the **Close** button (■) to exit the Windows Media Player window.

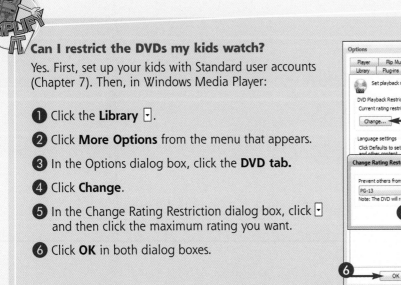

Can I restrict the DVDs my kids watch?

Yes. First, set up your kids with Standard user accounts (Chapter 7). Then, in Windows Media Player:

① Click the **Library** ▪.

② Click **More Options** from the menu that appears.

③ In the Options dialog box, click the **DVD tab.**

④ Click **Change**.

⑤ In the Change Rating Restriction dialog box, click ▪ and then click the maximum rating you want.

⑥ Click **OK** in both dialog boxes.

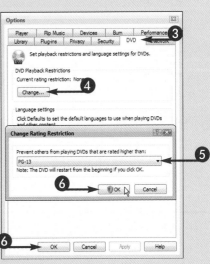

Navigate a DVD

You can control how a DVD plays by using the various navigation controls in the Windows Media Player window. The window includes volume and playback controls. You can also navigate to different scenes using the list of tracks in the Playlist pane. All scenes, or tracks, stem from a root menu that directs you to the DVD's contents.

Navigate a DVD

STOP AND START A DVD

1 Click the **Stop** button (■).

Windows Media Player stops the DVD playback.

2 Click the **Play** button (▶).

Windows Media Player restarts the playback from the beginning.

You can also click the **Pause** button (II) to pause the playback if you want to resume playing in the same scene.

NAVIGATE SCENES

1 Click the **Previous** button (I◀◀).

Windows Media Player jumps you to the previous scene.

2 Click the **Next** button (▶▶I).

Windows Media Player jumps you to the next scene.

● You can also navigate directly to a scene in the playlist by double-clicking the scene you want to play.

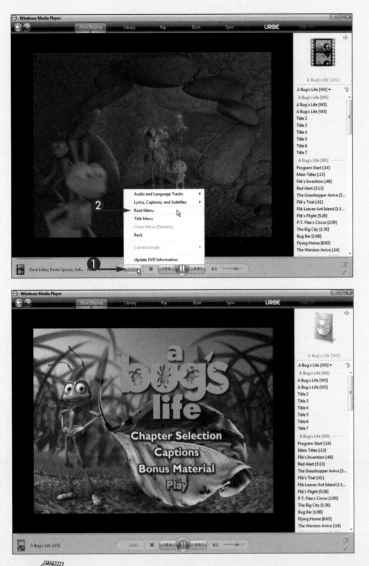

RETURN TO THE ROOT MENU

1 Click **DVD**.

2 Click **Root Menu**.

The DVD's opening menu appears in the Windows Media Player window.

What is a root menu?

The *root menu* is the opening menu of a DVD, and it typically displays links to the various segments, features, or clips on the DVD. You can return to the root menu at any time to access other DVD elements. You can quickly access the root menu with a shortcut menu. Right-click over the DVD screen, click **DVD Features**, and then click **Root Menu**.

Can I adjust the DVD's play speed?

Yes, you can choose from three settings: Slow, Normal, or Fast. The slow setting plays the DVD in slow motion. The normal setting plays the DVD at normal speed. The fast setting accelerates the play. To change the play speed, right-click the **Play** button (▶), and then click **Slow Playback** (or press Ctrl + Shift + S), **Normal Playback** (or press Ctrl + Shift + N), or **Fast Playback** (or press Ctrl + Shift + G).

Chapter 6

Working with Files

This chapter shows you how to work with the files on your computer. These easy and efficient methods show you how to view, select, copy, move, rename, and delete files, as well as how to copy files to a CD and how to create new folders to hold your files.

View Your Files

You can view the files you create, as well as those you download and copy to your computer that are stored on your hard drive. If you want to open or work with those files, you first need to view them.

View Your Files

1. Click **Start**.
2. Click your user name.

Windows Vista displays your user folder.

3. Double-click the folder you want to view.

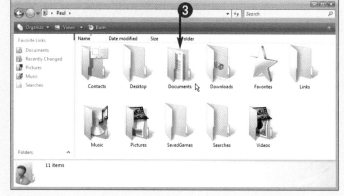

Windows Vista displays the contents of the folder including subfolders.

④ If the files you want to view are stored in a subfolder, double-click the subfolder.

Windows Vista displays the contents of the subfolder.

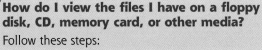
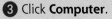

How do I view the files I have on a floppy disk, CD, memory card, or other media?

Follow these steps:

① Insert the floppy disk, CD, memory card, or removable media into the drive.

② Click **Start**.

③ Click **Computer**.

Windows Vista displays the Computer window.

④ Double-click the disk drive or device that contains the files you want to view.

Windows Vista displays the contents, including any subfolders.

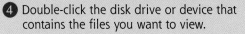

Select
a File

Although you learn specifically about selecting files in this task, the technique for selecting folders is exactly the same.

> Whether you want to rename a file, move several files to a new location, or delete some files, you first have to select the files so that Windows Vista knows exactly the ones with which you want to work.

Select a File

SELECT A SINGLE FILE

① Open the folder containing the file.

② Click the file.

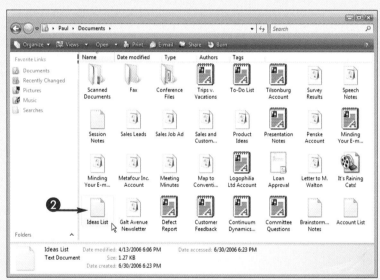

SELECT MULTIPLE FILES

① Open the folder containing the files.

② Click the first file you want to select.

③ Hold down **Ctrl** and click each of the other files you want to select.

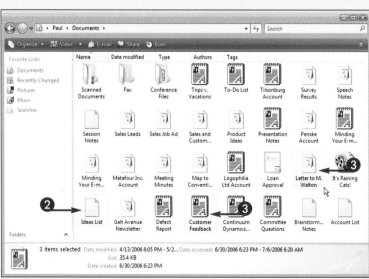

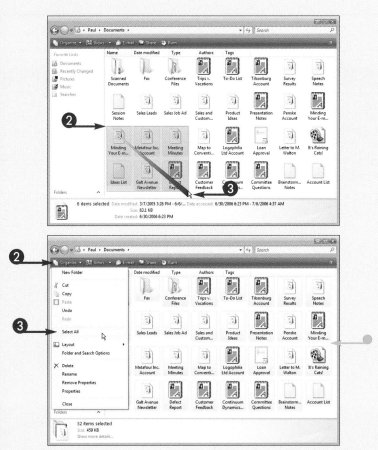

SELECT A GROUP OF FILES

❶ Open the folder containing the files.

❷ Position the mouse ⬚ slightly above and slightly to the left of the first file in the group.

❸ Click and drag the mouse ⬚ down and to the right until all the files in the group are selected.

SELECT ALL FILES

❶ Open the folder containing the files.

❷ Click **Organize**.

❸ Click **Select All**.

● Windows Explorer selects all the files in the folder.

Note: *A quick way to select all the files in a folder is to press* Ctrl *+* A *.*

How do I deselect a file?

● To deselect a single file from a multiple-file selection, hold down Ctrl and click the file you want to deselect.

● To deselect all files, click an empty area within the folder.

● To reverse the selection — deselect the selected files and select the deselected files — press Alt , click **Edit**, and then click **Invert Selection**.

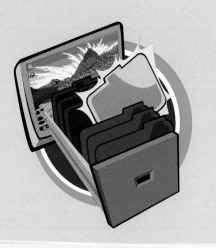

Change the File View

You can configure how Windows Vista displays the files in a folder by changing the file view. This enables you to see larger or smaller icons or the details of each file.

Choose a view such as Small Icons to see more files in the folder window. If you want to see more information about the files, choose either the Tiles view or Details view.

Change the File View

① Open the folder containing the files you want to view.

② Click the **Views** ⊡ to open the Views list.

③ Click the view you want.

● The slider points to the current view. You can also click and drag the slider to select a view.

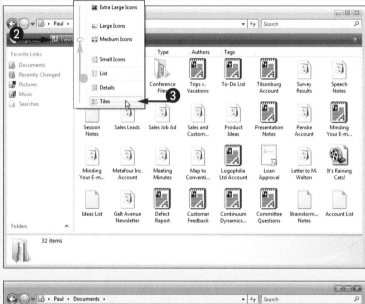

Windows Explorer changes the file view (to Tiles, in this example).

Preview a File

Windows Vista enables you to view the contents of some files without opening them. This makes it easier to select the file with which you want to work.

Windows Vista only previews certain types of files, such as text documents, rich text documents, Web pages, images, and videos.

Preview a File

1. Open the folder containing the file you want to preview.

2. Click the file.

3. Click **Organize**.

4. Click **Layout**.

5. Click **Preview Pane**.

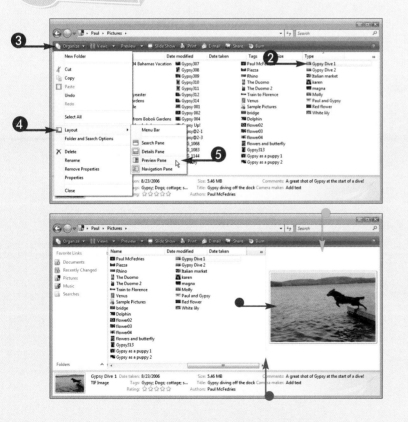

- The Preview pane appears.

- The file's contents appear in the Preview pane.

- Click and drag the left border of the Preview pane to change its size.

   When you are finished with the Preview pane, repeat Steps **3** to **5** to close it.

Copy
a File

You can make an exact copy of a file, which is useful if you want to make a backup of an important file on a floppy disk or on another removable disk, or if you want to send the copy on a disk to another person.

This task shows you how to copy a single file, but the steps also work if you select multiple files. You can also use these steps to copy a folder.

Copy a File

① Open the folder containing the file you want to copy.

② Select the file.

③ Press **Alt**.

● The Windows Explorer menu bar appears.

④ Click **Edit**.

⑤ Click **Copy To Folder**.

The Copy Items dialog box appears.

⑥ Click the location you want to use to store the copy.

● If the folder you want to use to store the copy is inside one of the displayed disk drives or folders, click here to display the location's folder, and then click the subfolder you want.

⑦ Click **Copy**.

Windows Vista copies the file.

Move a File

This task shows you how to move a single file, but the steps also work if you select multiple files. You can also use these steps to move a folder.

When you need to store a file in a new location, the easiest way is to move the file from its current folder to another folder on your computer.

Move a File

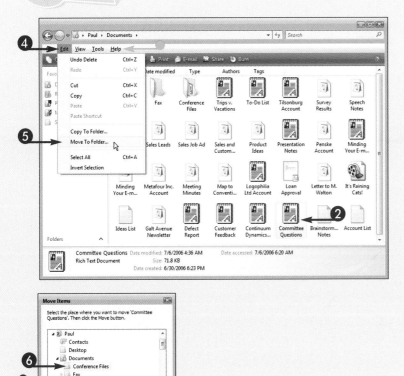

① Open the folder containing the file you want to move.

② Select the file.

③ Press **Alt**.

● The Windows Explorer menu bar appears.

④ Click **Edit**.

⑤ Click **Move To Folder**.

The Move Items dialog box appears.

⑥ Click the new location you want to use for the file.

● If the folder you want to use for the new location is inside one of the displayed disk drives or folders, click here to display the location's folder, and then click the subfolder you want.

⑦ Click **Move**.

Windows Vista moves the file.

Copy Files to a CD or DVD

If your computer has a recordable CD or DVD drive, you can copy files and folders to a recordable disc. This enables you to store a large amount of data in a single place for convenient transport, storage, or backup.

If you want to copy music files to a CD, see the "Burn Music Files to a CD" task in Chapter 5.

Copy Files to a CD or DVD

① Insert a recordable disc into your recordable CD or DVD drive.

A dialog box may appear asking what you want Windows to do with the disc.

② Click the **Close** button () to close the dialog box.

③ Open the folder containing the files you want to copy to the disc.

④ Select the files.

● To see how much data you are copying, read the Size number in the Details pane.

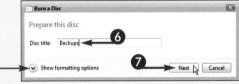

5 Click **Burn**.

Note: If you want to copy everything in the folder to the disc, do not select any file or folder and click Burn.

- If you have never used the disc for copying files, the Burn a Disc dialog box appears.

6 Type a title for the disc.

If you see a list of disc formats, click **Live File System** (◎ changes to ◉).

- If you do not see the formats, click **Show formatting options**.

7 Click **Next**.

Does it matter what type of recordable CD or DVD I use?
Not in Windows Vista. Normally, CD-R and DVD-R discs enable you to copy files to the disc only once. After you finalize the disc, it is locked and you cannot copy more files to it. Also, you cannot delete files from CD-R and DVD-R discs. However, Windows Vista uses a new system that enables you to copy, recopy, and delete files with any type of recordable disc.

How much data can I store on a recordable CD?
Most recordable CDs can hold about 650 MB (megabytes) of information. If a typical word processing document is about 50 KB (kilobytes), this means you can store about 13,000 files on a recordable CD. For larger files, such as images, you can store about 650 1 MB files on the disc.

Copy Files to a CD or DVD *(continued)*

With Windows Vista's new method for burning files to a CD or DVD, you only need to format the disc once. After that, you can burn more files to the disc, delete files from the disc, and more.

Copy Files to a CD or DVD *(continued)*

Windows Vista formats the disc and displays a dialog box to show you the progress.

When the format is complete, the Formatting dialog box disappears.

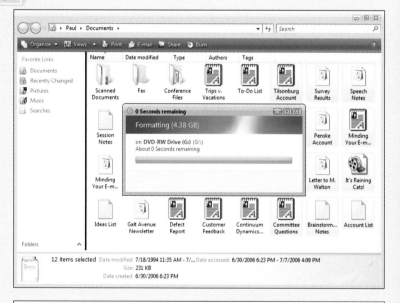

Windows Vista copies the files.

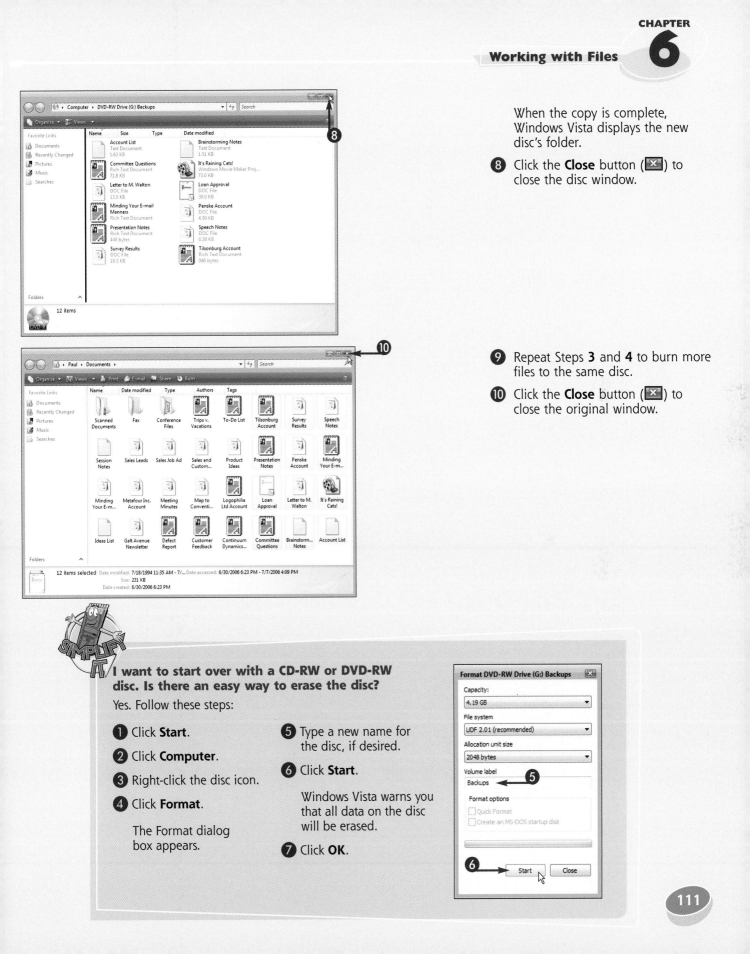

When the copy is complete, Windows Vista displays the new disc's folder.

⑧ Click the **Close** button (![x]) to close the disc window.

⑨ Repeat Steps **3** and **4** to burn more files to the same disc.

⑩ Click the **Close** button (![x]) to close the original window.

Rename a File

You can change the names of your files, which is useful if the current name of the file does not accurately describe its contents. By giving your documents descriptive names, you make it easier to later find the file you want.

Make sure that you only rename those documents that you have created yourself or that have been given to you by someone else. Do not rename any of the Windows Vista system files or any files associated with your programs, or your computer may behave erratically or crash.

Rename a File

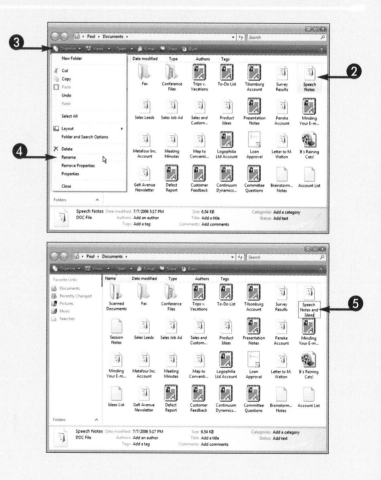

① Open the folder that contains the file you want to rename.

② Click the file.

③ Click **Organize**.

Note: In addition to renaming files, you can also rename any folders that you created yourself.

④ Click **Rename**.

A text box appears around the File name.

Note: You can also select the **Rename** command by clicking the file and then pressing F2.

⑤ Type the new name you want to use for the file.

Note: If you decide that you do not want to rename the file after all, press Esc to cancel the operation.

Note: The name you type can be up to 255 characters long, but it cannot include the following characters: < > , ? : " \ *

⑥ Press Enter or click an empty section of the folder.

The new name appears under the file's icon.

Create a New File

Create a New File

CHAPTER 6

You can quickly create a new file directly within a file folder. This method is faster, and often more convenient, than running a program's New command, as explained in the "Create a Document" task in Chapter 3.

Create a New File

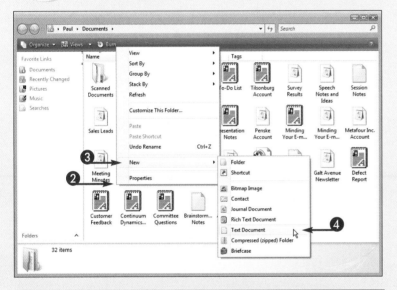

1 Open the folder in which you want to create the file.

2 Right-click an empty section of the folder.

3 Click **New**.

4 Click the type of file you want to create.

Note: If you click **Folder**, Windows Vista creates a new subfolder.

Note: The New menu on your system may contain more items than you see here because some programs install their own file types.

An icon for the new file appears in the folder.

5 Type the name you want to use for the new file.

6 Press Enter.

113

Delete a File

When you have a file that you no longer need, rather than leaving the file to clutter your hard drive, you can delete it.

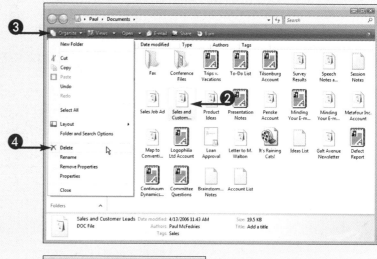

Make sure that you only delete those documents that you have created yourself or that have been given to you by someone else. Do not delete any of the Windows Vista system files or any files associated with your programs, or your computer may behave erratically or crash.

Delete a File

1 Open the folder that contains the file you want to delete.

2 Click the file you want to delete.

Note: *If you need to remove more than one file, select all the files you want to delete.*

3 Click **Organize**.

4 Click **Delete**.

Note: *Another way to select the* **Delete** *command is to press* Delete .

- The Delete File dialog box appears.

5 Click **Yes**.

The file disappears from the folder.

Note: *Another way to delete a file is to click and drag it to the desktop Recycle Bin icon.*

Restore a Deleted File

You can restore a deleted file because Windows Vista stores each deleted file in a special folder called the Recycle Bin, where the file stays for a few days or a few weeks, depending on how often you empty the bin or how full the folder becomes.

If you delete a file in error, Windows Vista enables you to restore the file by placing it back in the folder from which you deleted it.

Restore a Deleted File

① Double-click the desktop **Recycle Bin** icon.

The Recycle Bin folder appears.

② Click the file you want to restore.

③ Click **Restore this item**.

The file disappears from the Recycle Bin and reappears in its original folder.

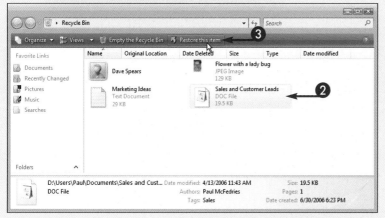

Search for a File

After you have used your computer for a while and have created many documents, you might have trouble locating a specific file. You can save a great deal of time by having Windows Vista search for your document.

You can search from the Start menu or use the Search box in a folder window.

Search for a File

SEARCH FROM THE START MENU

① Click **Start**.

② Click in the Search box.

③ Type your search text.

● As you type, Windows Vista displays the programs, documents, and other data on your system with a name that matches your search text.

④ If you see the program or document you want, click it to open it.

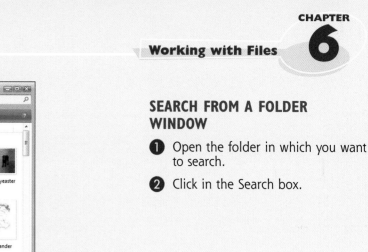

SEARCH FROM A FOLDER WINDOW

1 Open the folder in which you want to search.

2 Click in the Search box.

3 Type your search text.

● As you type, Windows Vista displays the folders and documents in the current folder with names, contents, or keywords that match your search text.

4 If you see the folder or document you want, double-click it to open it.

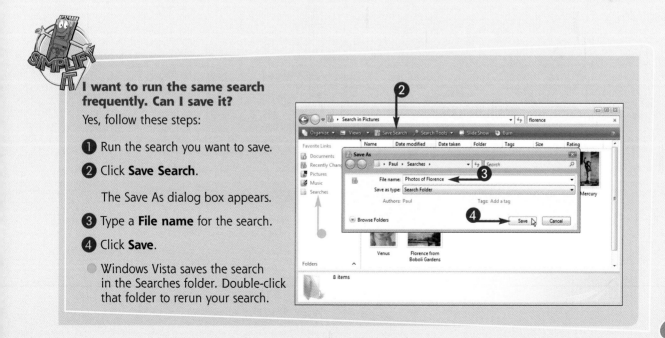

I want to run the same search frequently. Can I save it?

Yes, follow these steps:

1 Run the search you want to save.

2 Click **Save Search**.

The Save As dialog box appears.

3 Type a **File name** for the search.

4 Click **Save**.

● Windows Vista saves the search in the Searches folder. Double-click that folder to rerun your search.

Extract Files from a Compressed Folder

If someone sends you a file via e-mail, or if you download a file from the Internet, the file often arrives in a *compressed* form, which means the file actually contains one or more files that have been compressed to save space. To use the files on your computer, you need to extract them from the compressed file.

Because a compressed file can contain one or more files, it acts like a kind of folder. Therefore, Windows Vista calls such files *compressed folders, zipped folders,* or *ZIP archives.*

Extract Files from a Compressed Folder

1. Open the folder containing the compressed folder.

2. Right-click the compressed folder.

3. Click **Extract All**.

   Note: *You may not see the* **Extract All** *command if you have installed some other compression program such as WinZip.*

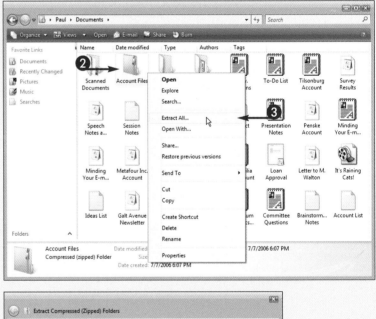

The Select a Destination screen of the Extraction Wizard appears.

4. Type the location of the folder into which you want the files extracted.

● You can also click **Browse** and choose the folder using the Select a Destination dialog box.

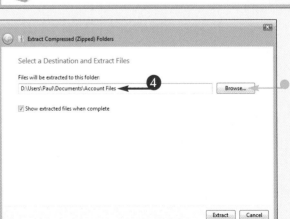

⑤ If you want to open the folder into which you extracted the files, click **Show extracted files when complete** (☐ changes to ☑).

⑥ Click **Extract**.

Windows Vista extracts the files.

Note: *You can view the contents of a compressed folder before you extract the files. Double-click the compressed folder to open it. Windows Vista treats the compressed folder just like a regular subfolder, which means it displays the files in their window. You can also extract the files in the compressed folder by clicking* **Extract all files** *in the Task pane.*

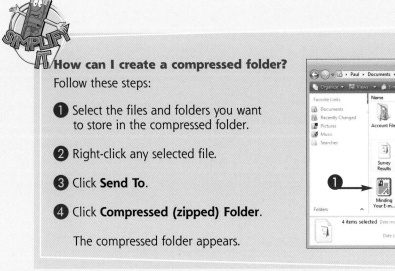

How can I create a compressed folder?

Follow these steps:

① Select the files and folders you want to store in the compressed folder.

② Right-click any selected file.

③ Click **Send To**.

④ Click **Compressed (zipped) Folder**.

The compressed folder appears.

Chapter 7

Sharing Your Computer with Others

If you share your computer with other people, you can create separate user accounts so that each person works only with his own documents, programs, and Windows Vista settings. This chapter shows you how to create and change user accounts, how to log on and off different accounts, how to share documents between accounts, and how to connect and work with a network.

Display User Accounts

To create, change, or delete user accounts, you need to display Windows Vista's Manage Accounts window.

A *user account* is a collection of Windows Vista folders and settings associated with one person.

Display User Accounts

① Click **Start**.

② Click **Control Panel**.

The Control Panel window appears.

③ Click **Add or remove user accounts**.

Note: If the User Account Control dialog box appears, click **Continue** or type an administrator password and click **Submit**.

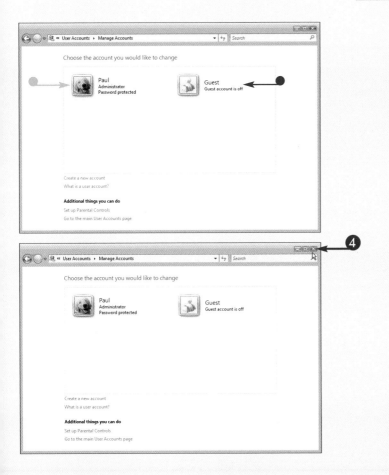

The Manage Accounts window appears.

● An Administrator account is created when you install Windows Vista. When you start Windows Vista, you log on with this account.

● The Guest account is also created when you install Windows Vista, but is turned off by default. The Guest account is a limited permission account that enables a person who does not have an account to use the computer. To turn on the Guest account, click **Guest**, and then click **Turn On**.

④ When you have finished working with user accounts, click the **Close** button (■) to close the Manage Accounts window.

How do user accounts help me share my computer with other people?
Without user accounts, anyone who uses your computer can view and even change your documents, Windows Vista settings, e-mail accounts and messages, Internet Explorer favorites, and more.

With user accounts, users get their own folders (Documents, Pictures, Music, and so on), personalized Windows Vista settings, e-mail accounts, and favorites. In short, users get their own versions of Windows Vista to personalize without interfering with anyone else's.

Create a User Account

Note that you must be logged on to Windows Vista with an administrator account or know an administrator's password to create a user account.

If you want to share your computer with another person, you need to create a user account for that individual.

Create a User Account

① Display the Manage Accounts window.

② Click **Create a new account**.

The Create New Account window appears.

③ Type the name you want to use for the new account.

④ Click the account type you want (◯ changes to ◉).

5 Click **Create Account**.

● The new account appears in the User Accounts window.

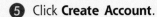

How do I decide what type of account to give each user?

The two different account types — administrator and standard — affect the extent to which the user can interact with the computer:

● An administrator has complete access to the computer, including access to all users' documents. Administrators can also install programs and devices and add, change, and delete user accounts.

● Standard users have partial access to the computer. They can access only their own documents, as well as any documents that other users have designated to share. Standard users can modify only their own settings, and can change some aspects of their user accounts, including their passwords and pictures.

Switch Between Accounts

Windows Vista leaves the original user's programs and windows running so that after the second person is finished, the original user can log on again and continue working as before.

After you have created more than one account on your computer, you can switch between accounts. This is useful when one person is already working in Windows Vista and another person needs to use the computer.

Switch Between Accounts

❶ Click **Start**.

● The current user's name and picture appear on the Start menu.

❷ Click here to display the menu.

❸ Click **Switch User**.

The Welcome screen appears.

❹ Click the name of the user account to which you want to switch.

- If the account is protected by a password, the password box appears.

  Note: See the "Protect an Account with a Password" task later in this chapter for details on protecting an account with a password.

⑤ Type the password.

⑥ Click the **Go** arrow ().

⑦ Click **Start**.

- The user's name and picture now appear in the Start menu.

What happens if I forget my password?
When you set up your password, Windows Vista asked you to supply a hint to help you remember the password. If you cannot remember your password, type anything into the password text box and click the **Go** arrow (➡). When Windows Vista tells you the password is incorrect, click **OK** to return to the Welcome screen and see the password hint.

Change a User's Name

> If the user name you are using now is not suitable for some reason, you can change it to a different name.

Change a User's Name

1 Display the Manage Accounts window.

2 Click the user account with which you want to work.

The Change an Account window appears.

3 Click **Change the name**.

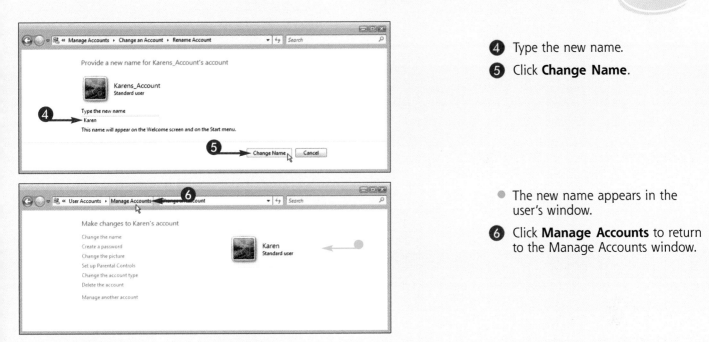

④ Type the new name.

⑤ Click **Change Name**.

● The new name appears in the user's window.

⑥ Click **Manage Accounts** to return to the Manage Accounts window.

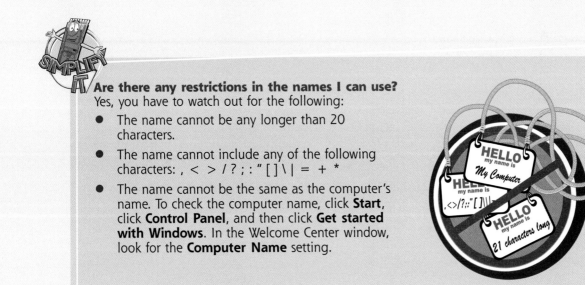

Are there any restrictions in the names I can use?
Yes, you have to watch out for the following:

● The name cannot be any longer than 20 characters.

● The name cannot include any of the following characters: , < > / ? ; : " [ ] \ | = + *

● The name cannot be the same as the computer's name. To check the computer name, click **Start**, click **Control Panel**, and then click **Get started with Windows**. In the Welcome Center window, look for the **Computer Name** setting.

Protect an Account with a Password

You can protect your account with a password. This is often a good idea because otherwise another user can log on to your account just by clicking your user name in the Welcome screen.

① Display the Manage Accounts window.

② Click the user account with which you want to work.

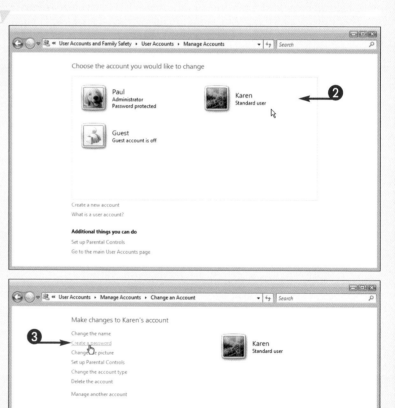

The Change an Account window appears.

③ Click **Create a password**.

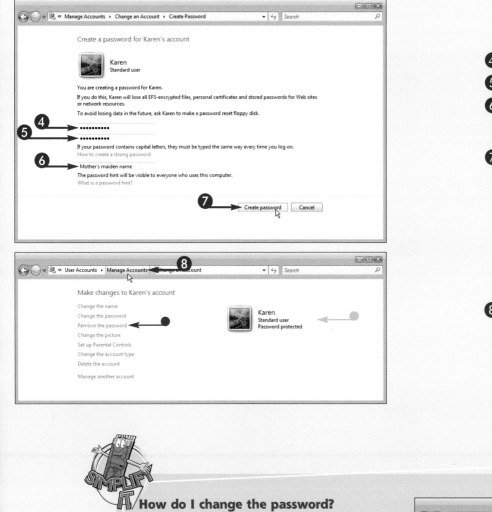

The Create Password window appears.

④ Type the password.

⑤ Type the password again.

⑥ Type a word or phrase to use as a password hint in case you forget the password.

⑦ Click **Create password**.

● The user's window appears and indicates that the account is now password protected.

⑧ Click **Manage Accounts** to return to the Manage Accounts window.

● To remove the password, click the user account and then click **Remove the password**. Read the details in the Remove Password window and then click **Remove Password**.

SIMPLIFY IT

How do I change the password?

Follow these steps:

① Click the user account with which you want to work.

② Click **Change the password**.

③ Type the password.

④ Type the password again.

⑤ Type a word or phrase to use as a password hint in case you forget the password.

⑥ Click **Change password**.

Delete an Account

You can delete a user's account when it is no longer needed. This reduces the number of users on the Manage Accounts and Welcome screens and can free up some disk space.

Delete an Account

① Display the Manage Accounts window.

② Click the user account you want to delete.

The Change an Account window appears.

③ Click **Delete the account**.

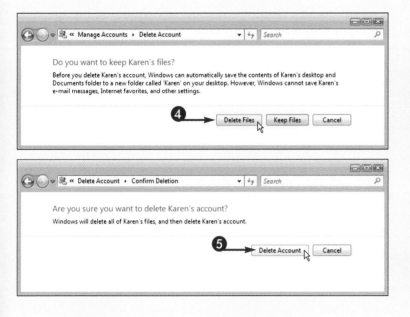

The Delete Account window appears.

④ Click to specify whether you want to keep or delete the user's personal files.

The Confirm Deletion window appears.

⑤ Click **Delete Account**.

Windows Vista deletes the account.

My user account does not offer the Delete the account task. Why not?
If yours is the only computer administrator account left on the computer, Windows Vista will not allow you to delete it. Windows Vista requires that there always be at least one computer administrator account on the computer.

What is the difference between the Keep Files and Delete Files options?
The options enable you to handle user files two ways:

● Click **Keep Files** to retain the user's personal files — the contents of his or her Documents folder and desktop. These files are saved on your desktop in a folder named after the user. All other personal items — settings, e-mail accounts and messages, and Internet Explorer favorites — are deleted.

● Click **Delete Files** to delete all of the user's personal files, settings, messages, and favorites.

Set Up Parental Controls

Before you can apply parental controls, you must set up a Windows Vista user account for each child (or one account for all the children). See the "Create a User Account" task earlier in this chapter.

If your children have computer access, you can protect them from malicious content by setting up parental controls for activities such as surfing the Web, playing games, and running programs.

Set Up Parental Controls

ACTIVATE PARENTAL CONTROLS

1. Click **Start**.
2. Click **Control Panel**.

The Control Panel window appears.

3. Click **Set up parental controls for any user**.

Note: If the User Account Control dialog box appears, click **Continue** or type an administrator password and click **Submit**.

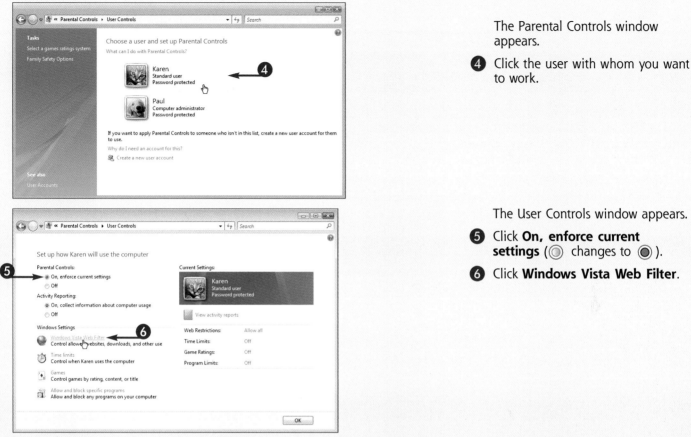

The Parental Controls window appears.

④ Click the user with whom you want to work.

The User Controls window appears.

⑤ Click **On, enforce current settings** (◎ changes to ◉).

⑥ Click **Windows Vista Web Filter**.

Is there any way to monitor my kids' computer activities?
Yes. In the User Controls window, click **On, collection information about computer usage** (◎ changes to ◉). Later you can view an activity summary by clicking **Activity reports**. The Activity Report window shows the user's most visited and recently visited Web sites, file downloads, logon times, programs and games used, instant messaging activity, the number of e-mails sent and received, and more.

How do I prevent my kids from downloading files?
Blocking downloads is a good idea because it reduces the risk of infecting the computer with viruses or other malicious software. In the User Controls window, click **Windows Vista Web Filter** to display the Web Restrictions window, shown on the next page. Scroll down to the bottom of the window and click **Block file downloads** (☐ changes to ☑). Click **OK**.

continued

Set Up Parental Controls *(continued)*

With parental controls activated, you can now set up specific restrictions. For Web surfing, you can block sites and content not suitable for children. You can also set up times when children are not allowed to use the computer.

Windows Vista's parental controls also enable you to set the maximum game rating that kids can play and block specific programs.

Set Up Parental Controls *(continued)*

SET WEB RESTRICTIONS

The Web Restrictions window appears.

7 Click **Block some websites or content** (◯ changes to ◉).

● If you want to control specific sites, click **Edit the Allow and block list**, type the site address, and then click **Allow** or **Block**.

8 Click a Web restriction level (◯ changes to ◉).

9 If you clicked **Custom**, click the check box for each category you want to block (☐ changes to ☑).

10 Click **OK**.

SET COMPUTER TIME LIMITS

● The Web Restrictions setting now shows the current Web restriction level.

11 Click **Time limits**.

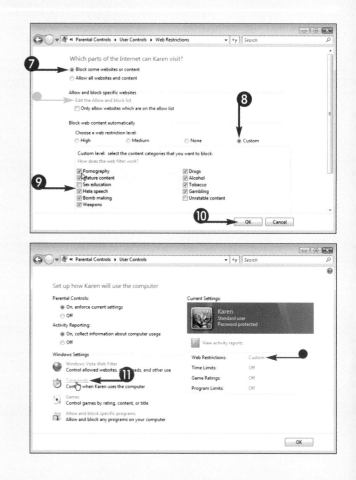

Control when Karen will use the computer

Click and drag the hours you want to block or allow.

	Midnight (AM)												Noon (PM)											
	12	1	2	3	4	5	6	7	8	9	10	11	12	1	2	3	4	5	6	7	8	9	10	11	12
Sunday																								
Monday																								
Tuesday																								
Wednesday																								
Thursday																								
Friday																								
Saturday																								

☐ Allowed
☐ Blocked

OK   Cancel

Parental Controls ▸ User Controls

Set up how Karen will use the computer

Parental Controls:
◉ On, enforce current settings
○ Off

Activity Reporting:
◉ On, collect information about computer usage
○ Off

Windows Settings

Windows Vista Web Filter
Control allowed websites, downloads, and other use

Time limits
Control when Karen uses the computer

Current Settings:

Karen
Standard user
Password protected

View activity reports

Web Restrictions:	Custom
Time Limits:	On
Game Ratings:	Off
Program Limits:	Off

OK

The Time Restriction window appears.

⑫ Click each hour that you want to block access to the computer.

● Blocked hours appear in blue.

● Allowed hours appear in white.

Note: *To block out a number of hours over a number of days, click and drag the mouse ⌖ over the hours.*

⑬ Click **OK**.

● The Time Limits setting now shows On.

⑭ Click **OK**.

How do I restrict game usage?
Windows Vista supports the game ratings supplied by the Entertainment Software Rating Board. In the User Controls window, click **Games** and then click **Set game ratings** to display the Game Restrictions window. Click the maximum rating the user can play (○ changes to ◉). You can also click the check boxes to block specific types of content (☐ changes to ☑). Click **OK**.

Can I prevent my kids from running certain programs?
Yes. In the User Controls window, click **Allow or block specific programs** to display the Application Restrictions dialog box. Click **User can only use the programs I allow** (where *User* is the name of the user). In the list, click the check box for each program you want the user to be able to run (☐ changes to ☑). Click **OK**.

Surfing the World Wide Web

After you have your Internet connection up and running, you can use Windows Vista's Internet Explorer program to navigate — or surf — the sites of the World Wide Web. This chapter explains the Web and shows you how to navigate from site to site.

World Wide Web

Understanding the World Wide Web

The World Wide Web — the Web, for short — is a massive storehouse of information that resides on computers, called Web servers, located all over the world.

Web Page

World Wide Web information is presented on Web pages, which you download to your computer using a Web browser program, such as Windows Vista's Internet Explorer. Each Web page can combine text with images, sounds, music, and even video to present you with information on a particular subject. The Web consists of billions of pages covering almost every imaginable topic.

Web Site

A Web site is a collection of Web pages associated with a particular person, business, government, school, or organization. Web sites are stored on a Web server, a special computer that makes Web pages available for people to browse.

Web Address

Every Web page has its own Web address that uniquely identifies the page. This address is sometimes called a *URL* (pronounced *yoo-ar-ell* or *erl*), which is short for Uniform Resource Locator. If you know the address of a page, you can plug that address into your Web browser to view the page.

Links

A link (also called a hyperlink) is a kind of "cross-reference" to another Web page. Each link is a bit of text (usually shown underlined and in a different color) or an image that, when you click it, loads the other page into your Web browser automatically. The other page is often from the same site, but it is common to come across links that take you to pages anywhere on the Web.

Start Internet Explorer

You can use Internet Explorer, Windows Vista's built-in Web browser program, to surf the Web. To do this, you must first start Internet Explorer.

Start Internet Explorer

① Connect to the Internet.

② Click **Start**.

③ Click **Internet**.

*Note: If your computer is set up so that the Internet item on the Start menu launches some other browser, click **All Programs**, and then click **Internet Explorer**.*

The Internet Explorer window appears.

● When you are finished with the Web, click the **Close** button (⊠) to shut down Internet Explorer.

Navigate Internet Explorer

You can easily surf the Web if you know your way around the Internet Explorer Web browser.

Web Page Title
This part of the Internet Explorer title bar displays the title of the displayed Web page.

Address Bar
This text box displays the address of the displayed Web page. You can also use the Address bar to type the address of a Web page that you want to visit.

Links
Links appear either as text or as images. On most pages (although not the page shown here), text links appear underlined and in a different color (usually blue) than the regular page text.

Current Link
This is the link that you are currently pointing at with your mouse. The mouse pointer changes from ☖ to ☝. On some pages (such as the one shown here), the link text also becomes underlined and changes color.

Status Bar
This area displays the current status of Internet Explorer. For example, it displays ìOpening page" when you are downloading a Web page, and "Done" when the page is fully loaded. When you point at a link, the Status bar displays the address of the page associated with the link.

Select a Link

Knowing which words, phrases, or images are links is not always obvious. The only way to tell for sure in many cases is to position the ↖ over the text or image; if the ↖ changes to ☝, you know you are dealing with a link.

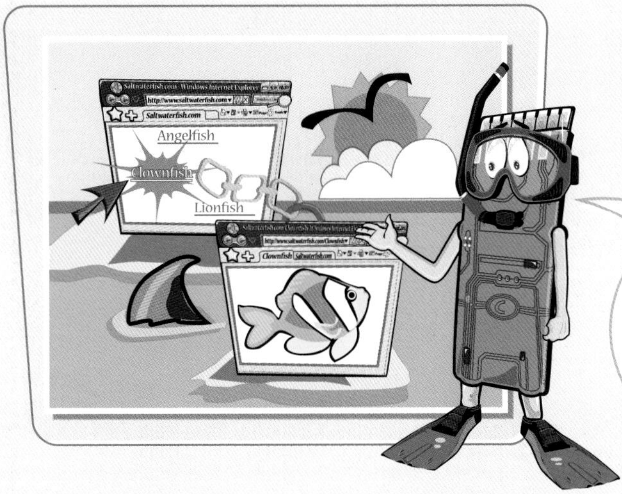

Almost all Web pages include links to other pages that contain information related to something in the current page, and you can use these links to navigate to other Web pages. When you select a link, your Web browser loads the other page.

Select a Link

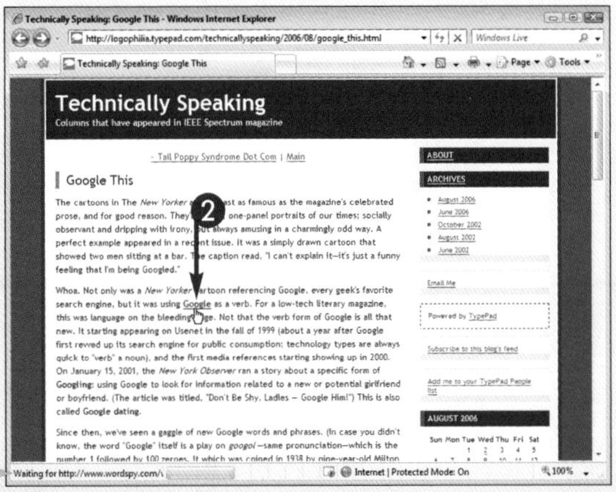

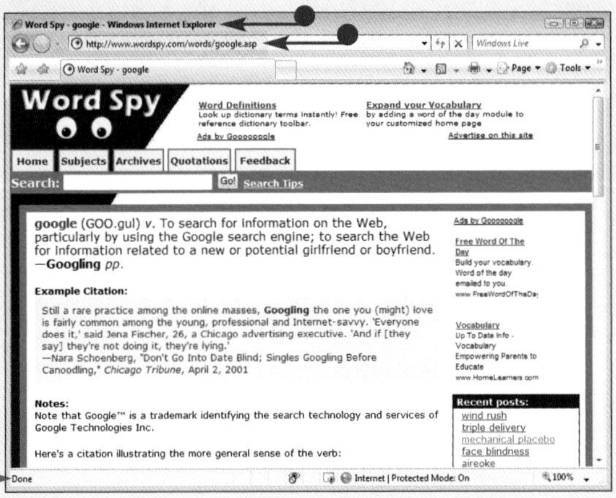

1. Position the ↖ over the link (↖ changes to ☝).
2. Click the text or image.

- The Status bar shows the current download status.

Note: ***The address shown in the Status bar when you point at a link may be different than the one shown when the page is downloading. This happens when the Web site "redirects" the link, which happens frequently.***

The linked Web page appears.

- The Web page title and address change after the linked page is loaded.
- The status bar shows Done when the page is completely loaded.

Enter a Web Page Address

If you know the address of a specific Web page, you can type that address into the Web browser and the program will display the page.

Enter a Web Page Address

1 Click in the Address bar.

2 Type the address of the Web page.

3 Click the **Go** arrow (➡) or press
Enter .

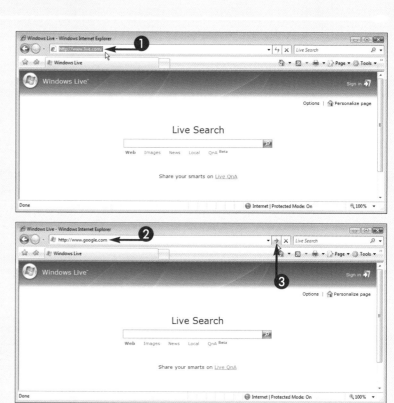

The Web page appears.

● The Web page title changes after the page is loaded.

REDISPLAY A WEB PAGE

1 Click the Address bar ⊡.

A list of the addresses you have typed appears.

2 Click the address you want to display.

The Web page appears.

Note: *If you type the first few letters of the address (such as **goog**), the Address bar displays a list of addresses that match what you have typed. If you see the address you want, click it to load the page.*

Are there any shortcuts I can use to enter Web page addresses?

Here are some useful keyboard techniques:

● After you finish typing the address, press `Enter` instead of clicking the **Go** arrow (➡).

● Most Web addresses begin with *http://*. You can leave off these characters when you type your address; Internet Explorer adds them automatically.

● If the address uses the form http://www.something.com, type just the "something" part and press `Ctrl` + `Enter`. Internet Explorer automatically adds *http://www.* at the beginning and *.com* at the end.

When I try to load a page, why does Internet Explorer tell me "The page cannot be displayed"?

This message means that Internet Explorer is unable to contact a Web server at the address you typed. This is often a temporary glitch, so click the **Go** arrow (➡) to try loading the page again. If the trouble persists, double-check your address to ensure that you typed it correctly. If you did, the site may be unavailable for some reason. Try again in a few hours.

Open a Web Page in a Tab

You can make it easier to work with multiple Web pages simultaneously by opening each page in its own tab.

You can open as many pages as you like in their own tabs. This is convenient because all the pages appear within a single Internet Explorer window.

Open a Web Page in a Tab

OPEN A WEB PAGE IN A TAB

1 Right-click the link you want to open.

2 Click **Open in New Tab**.

● A new tab appears with the page title.

3 Click the tab to display the page.

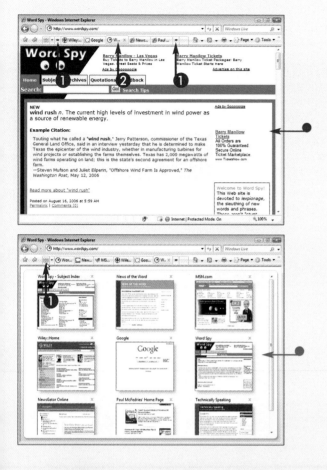

NAVIGATE TABS

1 Click the **Tab Left** button () or the **Tab Right** button () to display the tab you want.

Note: You only see the Tab Left and Tab Right buttons if Internet Explorer does not have enough room to display all the tabs.

2 Click the tab.

● The Web page loaded in the tab appears.

DISPLAY QUICK TABS

1 Click the **Quick Tabs** button (⊞).

● Internet Explorer displays thumbnail images of the Web pages open in each tab.

Are there any shortcuts I can use to open Web pages in tabs?

Here are some useful keyboard techniques:

● Hold down `Ctrl` and click a link to open the page in a tab.

● Hold down `Ctrl` + `Shift` and click a link to open the page in a tab and display the tab.

● Type an address and then press `Alt` + `Enter` to open the page in a new tab.

● Press `Ctrl` + `Q` to display the Quick Tabs.

● Press `Ctrl` + `Tab` or `Ctrl` + `Shift` + `Tab` to cycle through the tabs.

● Press `Ctrl` + `W` to close the current tab.

● Press `Ctrl` + `Alt` + `F4` to close every tab but the current one.

Navigate Web Pages

After you have visited several pages, you can return to a page you visited earlier. Rather than retyping the address or looking for the link, Internet Explorer gives you some easier methods.

When you navigate Web pages, you can go back to a page you have visited in the current browser session. After you have done that, you can also reverse course and go forward through the pages again.

Navigate Web Pages

GO BACK ONE PAGE

① Click the **Back** button (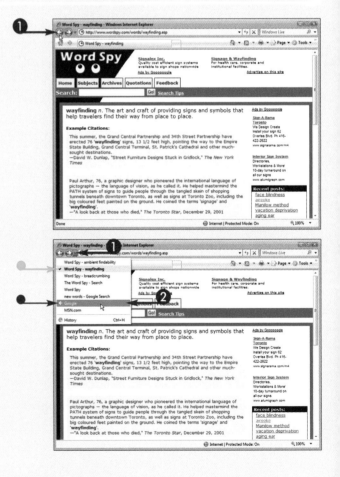).

The previous page you visited appears.

GO BACK SEVERAL PAGES

① Click the **Recent Pages** ⱽ.

A list of the sites you have visited appears.

● The current site appears with a check mark (☑) beside it.

● Items listed below the current site are ones you visited prior to the current site. When you hover the mouse ⬚ over a previous site, Internet Explorer displays the **Go Back** arrow (◀).

② Click the page you want to display.

The page appears.

GO FORWARD ONE PAGE

1 Click the **Forward** button (⊡).

The next page you visited appears.

*Note: If you are at the last page viewed up to that point, the **Forward** button (⊡) is not active.*

GO FORWARD SEVERAL PAGES

1 Click the **Recent Pages** ⊡.

A list of the sites you have visited appears.

● Items listed above the current site are ones you visited after the current site. When you hover the mouse ⊮ over a previous site, Internet Explorer displays the **Go Forward** arrow (⊡).

2 Click the page you want to display.

The page appears.

How do I go back or forward to a page, but also keep the current page on-screen?

You can do this by opening a second Internet Explorer window. Keep the current page in the original window and then use the second window to go back or forward. Here are the steps to follow:

1 Press **Ctrl** + **N**.

● A copy of the Internet Explorer window appears.

2 Use the techniques you learned in this task to navigate to the page you want.

Change Your Home Page

In the Windows Vista version of Internet Explorer, you can have a single home page or you can have multiple home pages that load in separate tabs each time you start the program.

Your home page is the Web page that appears when you first start Internet Explorer. The default home page is usually the Live.com site, but you can change that to any other page you want.

Change Your Home Page

CHANGE A SINGLE HOME PAGE

① Display the Web page that you want to use as your home page.

② Click the **Home** ⏷.

③ Click **Add or Change Home Page**.

The Change Home Page dialog box appears.

④ Click **Use this webpage as your only home page** (◯ changes to ◉).

⑤ Click **Yes**.

Internet Explorer changes your home page.

● You can click the **Home** button to display the home page at any time.

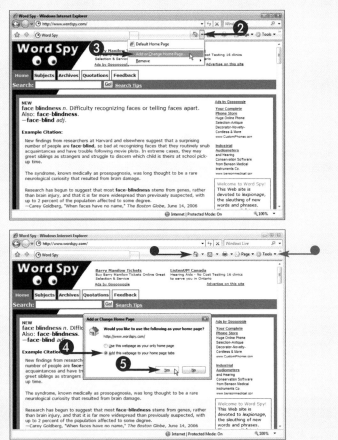

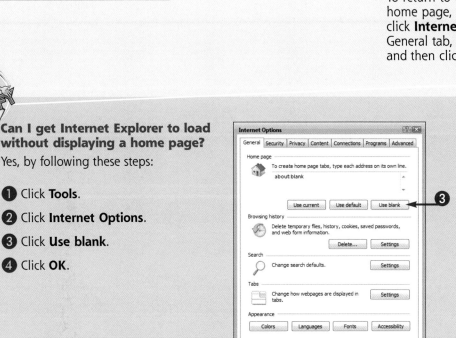

ADD A PAGE TO YOUR HOME PAGE TABS

1. Display the Web page that you want to add to your home page tabs.

2. Click the **Home** ⊡.

3. Click **Add or Change Home Page**.

The Change Home Page dialog box appears.

4. Click **Add this webpage to your home page tabs** (◯ changes to ◉)

5. Click **Yes**.

Internet Explorer adds the page to your home page tabs.

● You can click the **Home** button to display home page tabs at any time.

● To return to using your original home page, click **Tools** and then click **Internet Options**. In the General tab, click **Use default**, and then click **OK**.

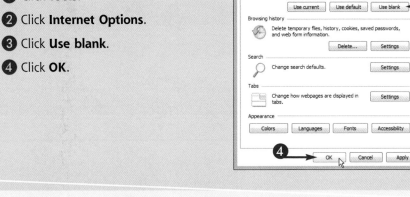

Can I get Internet Explorer to load without displaying a home page?

Yes, by following these steps:

1. Click **Tools**.

2. Click **Internet Options**.

3. Click **Use blank**.

4. Click **OK**.

Save Favorite Web Pages

The Favorites feature is a list of Web pages that you have saved. Rather than typing an address or searching for one of these pages, you can display the Web page by selecting its address from the Favorites list.

If you have Web pages that you visit frequently, you can save yourself time by saving those pages as favorites within Internet Explorer. This enables you to display the pages with just a couple of mouse clicks.

Save Favorite Web Pages

① Display the Web page you want to save as a favorite.

② Click the **Add to Favorites** button (⊞).

③ Click **Add to Favorites**.

The Add a Favorite dialog box appears.

Note: You can also display the Add a Favorite dialog box by pressing `Ctrl` + `D`.

④ Edit the page name, as necessary.

⑤ Click **Add**.

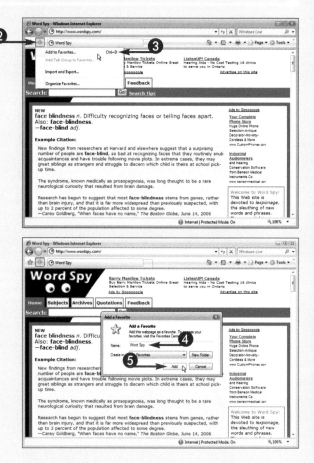

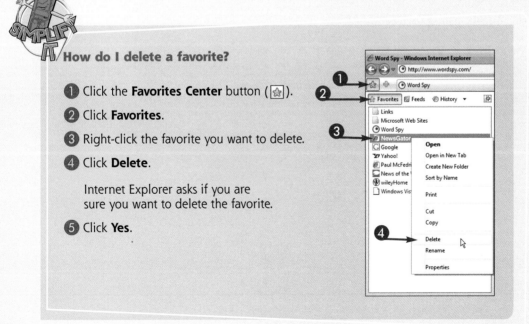

DISPLAY A FAVORITE WEB PAGE

1 Click the **Favorites Center** button (⭐).

2 Click **Favorites**.

The Favorites list appears.

3 Click the Web page you want to display.

The Web page appears.

● If you use the Favorites list a lot, you can make it easier way to display the pages by keeping the Favorites Center visible. Click the **Favorites Center** button (⭐) and then click the **Pin the Favorites Center** button (⬅). Internet Explorer pins the Favorites Center to the left side of the window.

How do I delete a favorite?

1 Click the **Favorites Center** button (⭐).

2 Click **Favorites**.

3 Right-click the favorite you want to delete.

4 Click **Delete**.

Internet Explorer asks if you are sure you want to delete the favorite.

5 Click **Yes**.

Search for Sites

If you need information on a specific topic, Internet Explorer has a built-in feature that enables you to quickly search the Web for sites that have the information you require.

The Web has a number of sites called *search engines* that enable you to find what you are looking for. By default, Internet Explorer uses the Live Search site, but you can use other sites.

Search for Sites

① Click in the **Instant Search** box.

② Type a word, phrase, or question that represents the information you want to find.

③ Click the **Search** button (🔍).

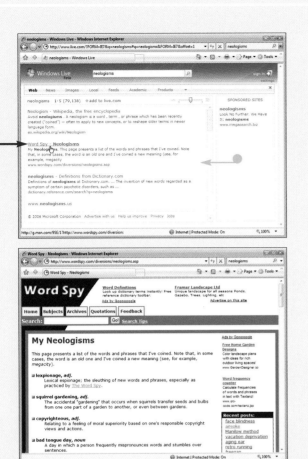

● A list of pages that match your search text appears.

④ Click a Web page.

The page appears.

Can I use other search engines?

Yes. To add another search engine, follow these steps:

❶ Click the search box ⊡.

❷ Click **Find More Providers**.

❸ Click the search engine you want to use.

❹ Click **Add Provider**.

To use the search engine, click the search box ⊡ and then click the search engine name.

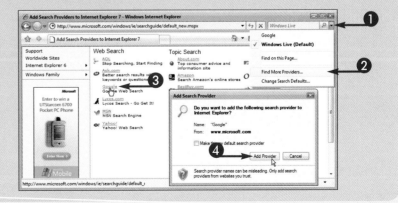

Chapter 9

Sending and Receiving E-mail

You can use Windows Vista's Windows Mail program to send e-mail to and read e-mail from friends, family, colleagues, and even total strangers almost anywhere in the world. This chapter shows you how to perform these and many more e-mail tasks.

Start Windows Mail

With Windows Mail, the e-mail program that comes with Windows Vista, you can send or receive e-mail messages. You must first launch Windows Mail.

Start Windows Mail

① Connect to the Internet.

② Click **Start**.

③ Click **E-mail**.

Note: If your computer is set up so that the E-mail item on the Start menu launches some other program, click **All Programs** and then click **Windows Mail**.

The Windows Mail window appears.

④ When you finish your e-mail chores, click the **Close** button (⊠) to shut down Windows Mail.

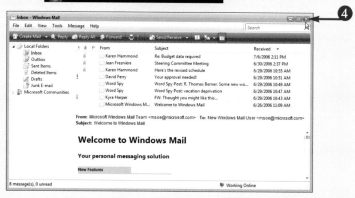

Navigate Windows Mail

Windows Mail makes e-mailing easy, but you can make it even easier by taking a few moments now to learn the layout of the Windows Mail window.

Instant Search
Type a word or phrase in this box to search for messages.

Messages
This area shows a list of the messages that are contained in the current folder.

Local Folders List
This area lists the six storage folders that Windows Mail provides. You use these folders to store various types of messages; you can also create your own folders. The six folders are:

Inbox stores your incoming messages. To learn how to get your messages, see the ìReceive and Read E-mail Messages" task in this chapter.

Outbox stores outgoing messages that you have not yet sent. To learn how to send messages, see the "Send an E-mail Message" task in this chapter.

Sent Items stores outgoing messages that you have sent.

Deleted Items stores messages that you have deleted from some other folder.

Drafts stores messages that you have saved but have not yet finished composing.

Junk E-mail stores messages that Windows Mail has determined to be spam.

Microsoft Communities
This item represents the newsgroups maintained by Microsoft. You can use these groups to ask questions about various Microsoft programs.

Preview Pane
This area shows a preview of the currently selected message.

Send an E-mail Message

If you do not know any e-mail addresses, or, if at first, you prefer to just practice sending messages, you can send messages to your own e-mail address.

If you know the e-mail address of a person or organization, you can send an e-mail message to that address. In most cases, the message is delivered within a few minutes.

Send an E-mail Message

1 Click **Create Mail**.

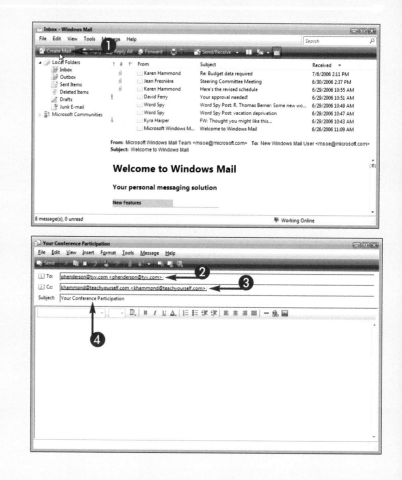

A message window appears.

2 Type the e-mail address of the person to whom you are sending the message.

3 To send a copy of the message to another person, type that person's e-mail address.

Note: You can add multiple e-mail addresses in both the To line and the Cc line. Separate each address with a semicolon (;).

4 Type a title or short description for the message.

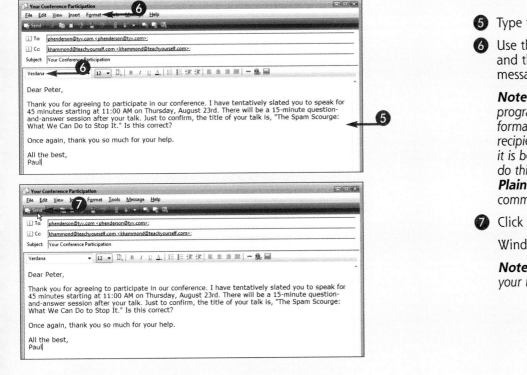

5 Type the message.

6 Use the buttons in the Formatting bar and the Format menu to format the message text.

Note: Many people use e-mail programs that cannot process text formatting. Unless you are sure your recipient's program supports formatting, it is best to send plain text messages. To do this, click **Format** and then click **Plain Text** (☑ appears beside the command).

7 Click **Send**.

Windows Mail sends your message.

Note: Windows Mail stores a copy of your message in the Sent Items folder.

I have a large number of messages to compose. Do I have to be online to do this?

No, composing all the messages while you are offline is possible. Follow these steps:

1 While disconnected from the Internet, start Windows Mail, and click **Cancel** if the program asks you to connect to the Internet.

2 To ensure you are working offline, click **File**. Click the **Work Offline** command if you do not see a check mark (☑) beside it.

3 Compose and send the messages. Each time you click **Send**, your messages are stored temporarily in the Outbox folder.

4 Connect to the Internet.

5 Click **File**.

6 Click **Work Offline**.

7 Click the **Send/Receive** ▾.

8 Click **Send All**.

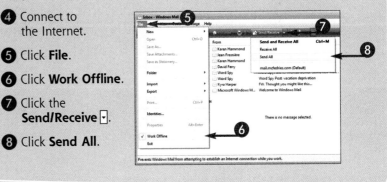

Add Someone to Your Contacts

You can use the Windows Vista Contacts folder to store the names and e-mail addresses of people with whom you frequently correspond.

When you choose a name from Contacts while composing a message, Windows Mail automatically adds the contact's e-mail address. This is faster and more accurate than typing the address by hand.

Add Someone to Your Contacts

① Click the **Contacts** button (📖).

You can also open the Contacts folder by pressing `Ctrl` + `Shift` + `C`, or by clicking **Start**, clicking **All Programs**, and then clicking **Windows Contacts**.

The Contacts window appears.

② Click **New Contact**.

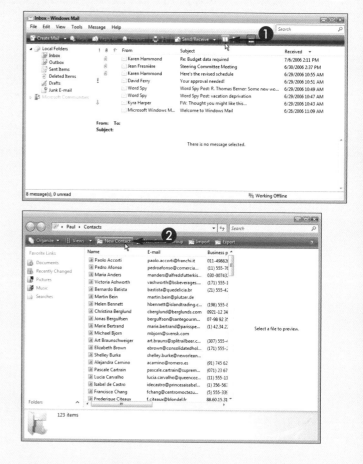

The Properties dialog box appears.

③ Type the person's first name.

④ Type the person's last name.

⑤ Type the person's e-mail address.

⑥ Click **Add**.

⑦ Click **OK**.

● Windows Vista adds the person to the Contacts list.

Note: *You can use the other tabs in the Properties dialog box to store more information about the contact, including home and business addresses and phone numbers, spouse and children names, birthday, and more.*

⑧ Click the **Close** button (◼) to close the Address Book window.

DELETE SOMEONE FROM YOUR CONTACTS

① Click the person's name that you want to delete.

② Click the **Organize** ⊡.

③ Click **Delete**. When Windows Vista asks you to confirm, click **Yes**.

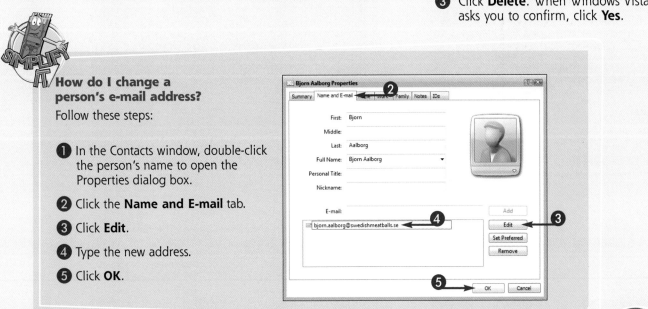

How do I change a person's e-mail address?

Follow these steps:

① In the Contacts window, double-click the person's name to open the Properties dialog box.

② Click the **Name and E-mail** tab.

③ Click **Edit**.

④ Type the new address.

⑤ Click **OK**.

Select a
Contact Address

After you have some e-mail addresses and names in your Contacts folder, when composing a message, you can select the address you want directly from Contacts instead of typing the address.

Select a Contact Address

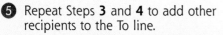

① Click **Create Mail** to start a new message.

② Click **To**.

The Select Recipients dialog box appears.

③ Click the person to whom you want to send the message.

④ Click **To**.

● The person's name appears in the Message recipients box.

⑤ Repeat Steps **3** and **4** to add other recipients to the To line.

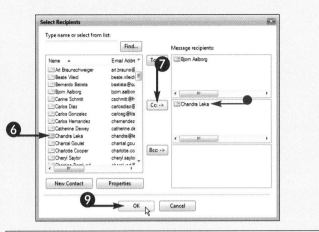

6 To send a copy of the message to a recipient, click the person's name.

7 Click **Cc**.

● The person's name appears in the Message recipients box.

8 Repeat Steps **6** and **7** to add other recipients to the Cc line.

9 Click **OK**.

● Windows Mail adds the recipients to the To and Cc lines of the new message.

● In the Select Recipients dialog box, click **Bcc** to add the current contact to the message Bcc field. Bcc stands for *blind courtesy copy*, and it means that any addresses in the Bcc field are not displayed to the other message recipients. You only see the Bcc field if you have added a Bcc recipient. Alternatively, click **View** and then click **All Headers** to display the Bcc field.

Can I send a message from my Contacts list?

Yes, and you do not even need to have Windows Mail running:

1 Open the Contacts folder.

2 Click the name of the person you want to send a message to.

3 Click **E-Mail**.

A new message appears with the recipient's name filled in automatically.

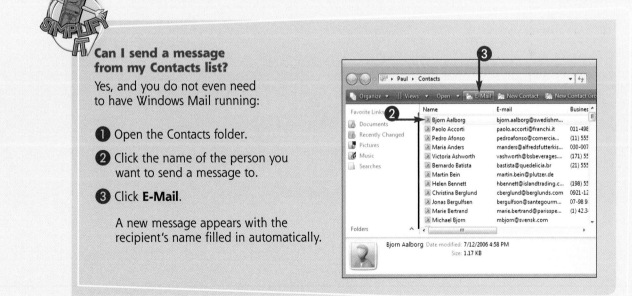

Add a File Attachment

If you have a memo, an image, or another document that you want to send to another person, you can attach the document to an e-mail message. The other person can then open the document after he or she receives your message.

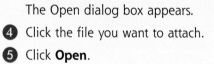

Add a File Attachment

❶ Click **Create Mail** to start a new message.

❷ Click **Insert**.

❸ Click **File Attachment**.

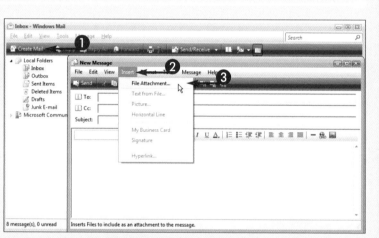

The Open dialog box appears.

❹ Click the file you want to attach.

❺ Click **Open**.

● Windows Mail attaches the file to the message.

6 Repeat Steps **2** to **5** to attach additional files to the message.

● You can also display the Open dialog box by clicking the **Attach File to Message** button (🖉).

ADD AN ATTACHMENT DIRECTLY

1 Open the folder that contains the file you want to send as an attachment.

2 Click the file.

3 Click **E-mail**.

Windows Mail creates a new message and attaches the file.

Is there a limit to the number of files I can attach to a message?

There is no practical limit to the number of files you can attach to the message. However, you should be careful with the total *size* of the files you send. If you or the recipient has a slow Internet connection, sending or receiving the message can take an extremely long time. Also, many Internet service providers (ISPs) place a limit on the size of a message's attachments, which is usually around 2MB. In general, use e-mail to send only a few small files at a time.

Add a Signature

Signatures usually contain personal contact information, such as your phone numbers, business address, and e-mail and Web site addresses. Some people supplement their signatures with wise or witty quotations.

In an e-mail message, a *signature* is a small amount of text that appears at the bottom of the message. Rather than typing this information manually, you can create the signature once and then have Windows Mail add the signature to any message you send automatically.

ADD A SIGNATURE

1 Click **Tools**.

2 Click **Options**.

The Options dialog box appears.

3 Click the **Signatures** tab.

4 Click **New**.

● Windows Mail adds a new signature.

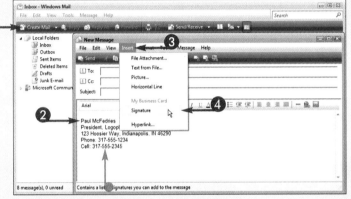

5 Type the signature text.

You can use these options to insert your signature automatically

- Click **Add signatures to all outgoing messages** (☐ changes to ☑) to have Windows Mail add your signature to the bottom of every new message.

- Click **Don't add signatures to Replies and Forwards** (☑ changes to ☐) if you want Windows Mail to add your signature when you reply to and forward messages.

6 Click **OK**.

INSERT THE SIGNATURE MANUALLY

1 Click **Create Mail** to start a new message.

2 In the message text area, move the insertion point to the location where you want the signature to appear.

3 Click **Insert**.

4 Click **Signature**.

Note: If you have more than one signature, click the one you want to use from the menu that appears.

- The signature appears in the message.

Can I have more than one signature?

Yes, you can add as many signatures as you want. For example, you may want to have one signature for business use and another for personal use. To give each signature a descriptive name, follow these steps:

1 In the Options dialog box, click the **Signature** tab.

2 Click the signature.

3 Click **Rename**.

4 Type the new name.

5 Press **Enter**.

Receive and Read E-mail Messages

Windows Mail checks for new messages when you start the program automatically, and then checks for more messages every 30 minutes while you are online.

A message sent to you by another person is stored on your ISP's e-mail server computer. You must connect to the ISP's computer to retrieve and read the message. As you see in this task, Windows Mail does most of the work for you automatically.

Receive and Read E-mail Messages

RECEIVE E-MAIL MESSAGES

1 Click the **Send Receive** ⋅.

2 Click **Receive All**.

- If you have new messages, they appear in your Inbox folder in bold type.

- Whenever a new message arrives, the **You Have New E-mail** icon appears in the taskbar's notification area.

- This symbol (🔖) means that the message came with a file attached.

- This symbol (➡) means the message was sent as high priority.

- This symbol (⬇) means the message was sent as low priority.

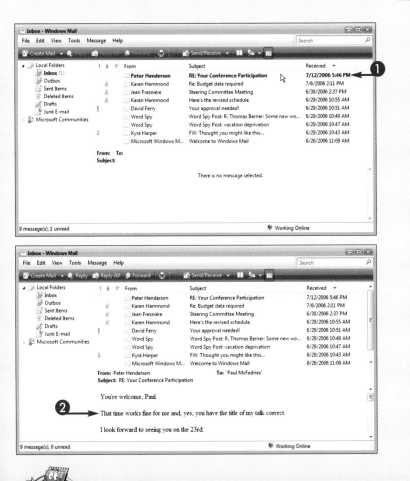

READ A MESSAGE

1 Click the message.

2 Read the message text in the preview pane.

Note: *If you want to open the message in its own window, double-click the message.*

Can I change how often Windows Mail automatically checks for messages?

Yes, by following these steps:

1 Click **Tools**.

2 Click **Options**.

The Options dialog box appears.

3 Click the **General** tab.

4 If you do not want Windows Mail to check for messages when the program starts, click **Send and receive messages at startup** (☑ changes to ☐).

5 Type a new time interval, in minutes, that you want Windows Mail to use when checking for new messages automatically.

6 Click **OK**.

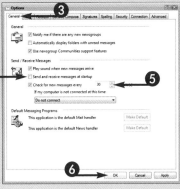

Reply to a Message

When a message you receive requires some kind of response — whether it is answering a question, supplying information, or providing comments or criticisms — you can reply to any message you receive.

Reply to a Message

1 Click the message to which you want to reply.

2 Click the reply type you want to use:

Click **Reply** to respond only to the first address displayed on the To line.

Click **Reply All** to respond to all the addresses in the To and Cc lines.

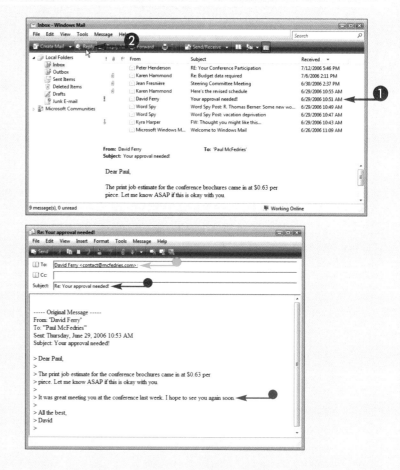

A message window appears.

● Windows Mail automatically inserts the recipient addresses.

● Windows Mail also inserts the subject line, preceded by Re.

● Windows Mail includes the original message's addresses (To and From), date, subject, and text at the bottom of the reply.

3 Edit the original message to include only the text that is relevant to your reply.

Note: *If the original message is fairly short, you usually do not need to edit the text. However, if the original message is long, and your response deals only with part of that message, you will save the recipient time by deleting everything except the relevant portion of the text.*

4 Click the area above the original message text and type your reply.

5 Click **Send**.

Windows Mail sends your reply.

Note: *Windows Mail stores a copy of your reply in the Sent Items folder.*

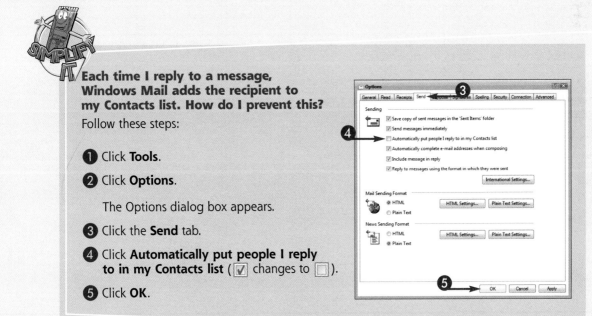

Each time I reply to a message, Windows Mail adds the recipient to my Contacts list. How do I prevent this?

Follow these steps:

1 Click **Tools**.

2 Click **Options**.

The Options dialog box appears.

3 Click the **Send** tab.

4 Click **Automatically put people I reply to in my Contacts list** (☑ changes to ☐).

5 Click **OK**.

Forward a Message

If a message has information that is relevant to or concerns another person, you can forward a copy of that message to the other recipient. You can also include your own comments in the forward.

Forward a Message

1 Click the message that you want to forward.

2 Click **Forward**.

A message window appears.

- Windows Mail inserts the subject line, preceded by Fw.

- The original message's addresses (To and From), date, subject, and text are included at the bottom of the forward.

3 Type the e-mail address of the person to whom you are forwarding the message.

4 To send a copy of the forward to another person, type that person's e-mail address in the Cc line.

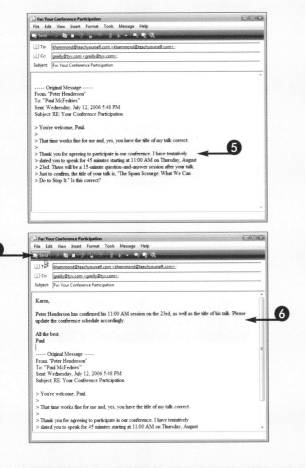

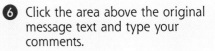

5 Edit the original message to include only the text that is relevant to your forward.

6 Click the area above the original message text and type your comments.

7 Click **Send**.

Windows Mail sends your forward.

Note: *Windows Mail stores a copy of your forward in the Sent Items folder.*

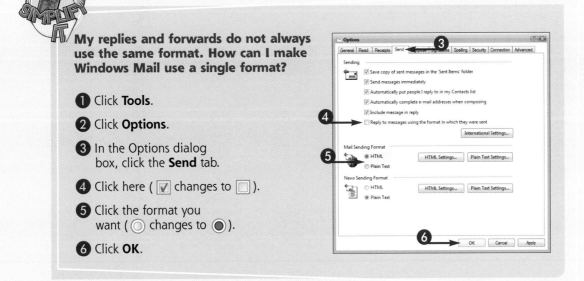

My replies and forwards do not always use the same format. How can I make Windows Mail use a single format?

1 Click **Tools**.

2 Click **Options**.

3 In the Options dialog box, click the **Send** tab.

4 Click here (☑ changes to ☐).

5 Click the format you want (○ changes to ◉).

6 Click **OK**.

Open and Save an Attachment

Be careful when dealing with attached files. Computer viruses are often transmitted by e-mail attachments.

If you receive a message that has a file attached, you can open the attachment to view the contents of the file. You can also save the attachment as a file on your computer.

Open and Save an Attachment

OPEN AN ATTACHMENT

1 Click the message that has the attachment, as indicated by the **Attachment** symbol (📎).

2 In the preview pane, click the **This message contains attachments** icon (📎).

A list of the message attachments appears.

3 Click the attachment you want to open.

Windows Mail asks you to confirm that you want to open the file.

4 Click **Open**.

The file opens in the appropriate program.

Note: *Instead of opening the file, Windows Vista may display a dialog box telling that the file "does not have a program associated with it." This means you need to install the appropriate program for the type of file. If you are not sure, ask the person who sent you the file what program you need.*

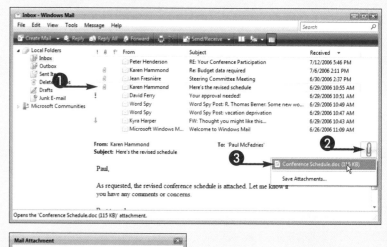

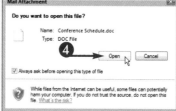

SAVE AN ATTACHMENT

① Click the message that has the attachment, as indicated by the **Attachment** symbol (⌀).

② In the preview pane, click the **This message contains attachments** icon (⌀).

A list of the message attachments appears.

③ Click **Save Attachments**.

The Save Attachments dialog box appears.

④ Click the file you want to save.

⑤ Type the name of the folder into which you want the file saved.

⑥ Click **Save**.

When I click This message contains attachments icon (⌀), why am I unable to click either the file name or the Save Attachments command?

Windows Mail has determined that the attached file may be unsafe, meaning that the file may harbor a virus or other malicious code. To confirm this, double-click the message to open it. Below the toolbar, you should see a message saying, "Windows Mail removed access to the following unsafe attachments in your mail." If you are certain the file is safe, turn off this feature by clicking **Tools** and then clicking **Options**, clicking the **Security** tab, and then clicking **Do not allow attachments to be saved or opened that could potentially be a virus** (☑ changes to ☐). Be sure to reactivate this feature after you have opened or saved the attachment.

Chapter 10

Tracking Appointments and Tasks

For most of us, life is busier than ever, and the number of appointments we have to keep and tasks we have to perform seems to increase daily. Fortunately, Windows Vista comes with a program that can help you manage your busy schedule. It is called Windows Calendar, and you can use it to enter and track appointments, all-day events, and tasks.

Start Windows Calendar

With Windows Calendar, the scheduling program that comes with Windows Vista, you can record appointments and tasks, set reminders for when these items are due, and more. To get started, you must first launch Windows Calendar.

Start Windows Calendar

① Click **Start**.

② Click **All Programs**.

③ Click **Windows Calendar**.

The Windows Calendar window appears.

④ When you finish your scheduling chores, click the **Close** button (❌) to shut down Windows Calendar.

Navigate Windows Calendar

Windows Calendar makes scheduling easy. However, you can make it even easier by taking some time now to learn the layout of the Windows Calendar window.

Date Navigator

This area shows the current month, and you use the Date Navigator to select the date on which you want to schedule an appointment, all-day event, or task. See the ìDisplay a Different Date" task, later in this chapter, to learn how to use the Date Navigator.

Appointment List

This area shows the appointments and all-day events that you have scheduled for whatever date is currently selected in the Date Navigator. The appointment list is divided into half-hour increments.

Details Pane

This area shows the details of the appointment or task that you are currently creating or editing.

Tasks

This area displays the list of tasks you have started but not yet completed.

Display a Different Date

Before you create an appointment or a task, you must first select the date on which the appointment occurs or the task begins.

Display a Different Date

USE THE DATE NAVIGATOR

① In the Date Navigator, click the **Next Month** button (▶) until the month of your appointment appears.

- If you go too far, click the **Previous Month** button (◀) to move back to the month you want.

- If you want to pick a month in the current year, click the current month and then click the month in the list that appears.

② Click the date.

- The date appears in the appointments list.

- If you want to return to today's date, click **Today**.

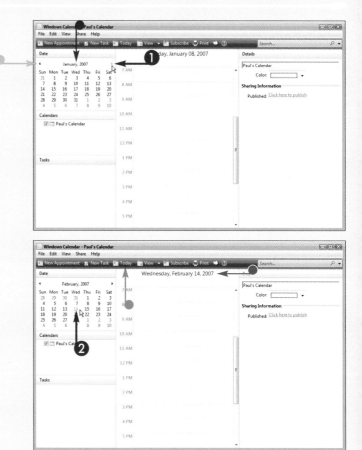

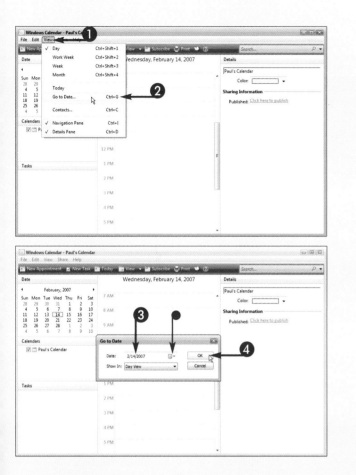

GO TO A SPECIFIC DATE

1 Click **View**.

2 Click **Go to Date**.

You can also select the Go to Date command by pressing Ctrl + G .

The Go to Date dialog box appears.

3 Use the Date text box to type the date you want using the format mm/dd/yyyy.

● You can also click here to display a Date Navigator that you can use to click the date you want.

4 Click **OK**.

Windows Vista displays the date in the appointments list.

Can I see more than one day at a time in the appointments list?
Yes. Click **View** and then click the view you want to use:

● **Day.** Shows the date that is currently selected in the Date Navigator. (You can also press Ctrl + Shift + 1 .)

● **Work Week.** Shows the work week (Monday through Friday) that includes the date that is currently selected in the Date Navigator. (You can also press Ctrl + Shift + 2).

● **Week.** Shows the full week that includes the date that is currently selected in the Date Navigator (You can also press Ctrl + Shift + 3 .)

● **Month.** Shows the month that includes the date that is currently selected in the Date Navigator. (You can also press Ctrl + Shift + 4 .)

View	
✓ Day	Ctrl+Shift+1
Work Week	Ctrl+Shift+2
Week	Ctrl+Shift+3
Month	Ctrl+Shift+4
Today	
Go to Date...	Ctrl+G
Contacts...	Ctrl+C
✓ Navigation Pane	Ctrl+I
✓ Details Pane	Ctrl+D

Create an Appointment

You can help organize your life by using Windows Calendar to record your appointments on the date and time they occur.

If the event has no set time — for example, a birthday, anniversary, or multiple-day event such as a sales meeting or vacation — you can create an all-day appointment.

Create an Appointment

① Navigate to the date when the appointment occurs.

② Click the time when the appointment occurs.

Note: If the appointment is more than half an hour, you can also click and drag the mouse ↳ over the full appointment period.

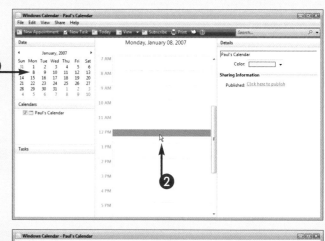

③ Click **New Appointment**.

Note: Another way to start a new appointment is to press **Ctrl** + **N**.

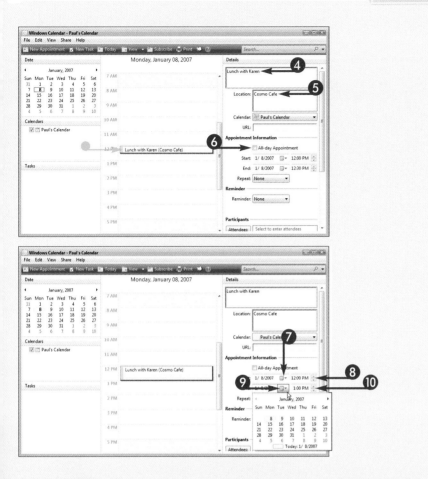

Windows Calendar adds a new appointment to the Details pane.

④ Type a name for the appointment.

⑤ Use the Location text box to type the appointment location.

● The appointment name and location appear in the Appointment list.

⑥ If the appointment is an anniversary or other event that lasts all day, click **All-day Appointment** (☐ changes to ☑).

⑦ If the start date is incorrect, use the Start date navigator to click the correct date.

⑧ If the start time is incorrect, use the Start time spin box to click the correct time.

⑨ If the end date is incorrect, use the End date navigator to click the correct date.

⑩ If the end time is incorrect, use the End time spin box to click the correct time.

Is there an easy way to schedule an appointment that occurs at a regular interval?

Yes, you can set up a recurring appointment. Windows Calendar can repeat an appointment daily, weekly, monthly, or yearly. You can also set up an advanced recurrence that uses a custom interval that you specify. Follow Steps **1** to **10** to set up a regular appointment. Click the **Repeat** ⬇, and then click the interval you want to use. Windows Calendar repeats the appointment at the interval you specified.

Can Windows Calendar remind me about an appointment?

Yes, you can specify a time interval before the appointment when Windows Calendar will display a dialog box to remind you of the appointment. You can set up the reminder to appear minutes, hours, days, or weeks before the appointment, or you can set the reminder to appear on a specific date. Follow Steps **1** to **10** to set up a regular appointment. Click the **Reminder** ⬇, and then click the interval you want to use. Windows Calendar configures the appointment to display a reminder.

Create a Task

When the task is done, you should mark it as complete so you can easily tell which tasks remain to be done.

You can monitor tasks — from large projects such as budgets to basic chores such as returning phone calls — by using Windows Calendar to record your tasks, including when they start and when they are due.

Create a Task

 Click **New Task**.

Note: Another way to start a new task is to press **Ctrl** + **T**.

Windows Calendar adds a new task to the Details pane.

2 Type a name for the task.

● The task name appears in the Tasks list.

3 Click the **Priority** ⦁ and then click the priority you want to assign the task.

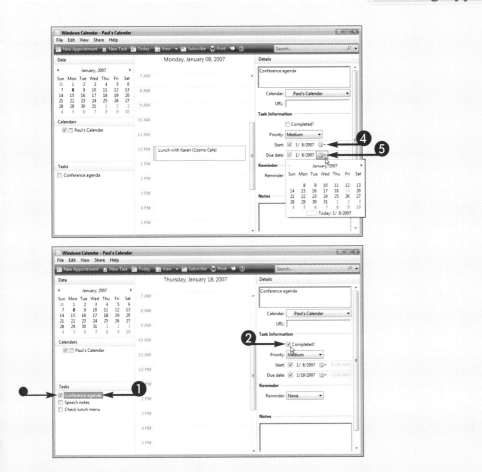

④ If the start date is incorrect, use the Start date navigator to click the correct date.

⑤ If the due date is incorrect, use the Due date navigator to click the correct date.

MARK A TASK AS COMPLETE

① Click the task.

② Click **Completed** (☐ changes to ☑).

● You can also click the task's check box in the Tasks list (☐ changes to ☑).

Can I organize the Tasks list with my highest priority items at the top?
Yes. The Tasks list is normally sorted by due date, but you can follow these steps to sort the list by priority:

① Right-click the Tasks list.

② Click **Sort by**.

③ Click **Priority**.

Windows Calendar sorts the tasks by priority, with the highest priority tasks at the top.

Can Windows Calendar remind me on a specific date and time when a task is due?
Yes. As with an appointment, you can specify a time interval before the task when Windows Calendar will display a dialog box to remind you of the task. You can also specify a specific date and time for the reminder:

① Follow Steps **1** to **5** to set up a task.

② Click the **Reminder** ⃕ and then click **On date**.

③ Type the date and time when you want the reminder to appear.

Windows Calendar configures the task to display a reminder.

Chapter 11

Customizing Windows Vista

Windows Vista comes with a number of features that enable you to personalize your computer. Not only can you change the appearance of Windows Vista to suit your taste, but you can also change the way Windows Vista works to make it easier to use and more efficient.

Open the Personalization Window

To make changes to many of Windows Vista's display options, you need to know how to open the Personalization window.

Open the Personalization Window

① Click **Start**.

② Click **Control Panel**.

The Control Panel window appears.

③ Click **Appearance and Personalization**.

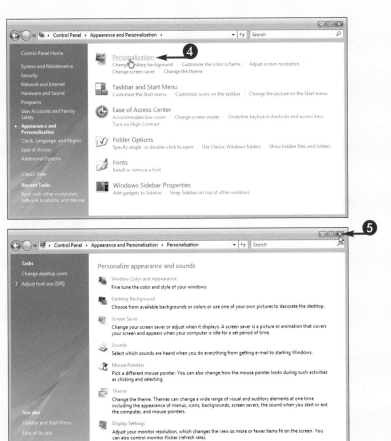

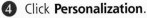

The Appearance and Personalization window appears.

④ Click **Personalization**.

The Personalization window appears.

⑤ Click the **Close** button (❌) when you are finished working with this window.

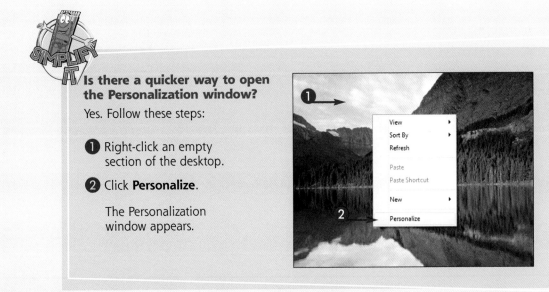

Is there a quicker way to open the Personalization window?

Yes. Follow these steps:

① Right-click an empty section of the desktop.

② Click **Personalize**.

The Personalization window appears.

View	▶
Sort By	▶
Refresh	
Paste	
Paste Shortcut	
New	▶
Personalize	

Change the Desktop Background

For a different look, you can change the desktop background to display either a different image or a specific color.

Change the Desktop Background

CHANGE THE BACKGROUND IMAGE

1 Open the Personalization window.

Note: See the "Open the Personalization Window" task earlier in this chapter.

2 Click **Desktop Background**.

The Desktop Background window appears.

3 Click ▼ and then click the background gallery you want to use.

Note: If you have your own image that you would prefer to use as the desktop background, click **Pictures** in the list. You can also click **Browse** and then use the Browse dialog box to select the file.

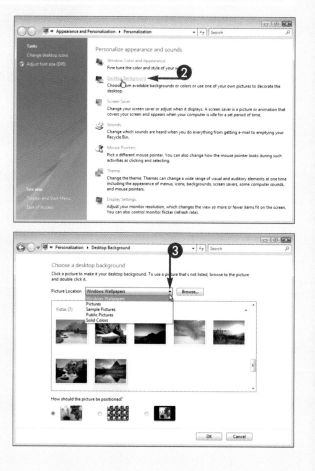

- Windows Vista displays the backgrounds in the selected gallery.

④ Click the image or color you want to use.

⑤ For an image, click the positioning option you want to use
(◯ changes to ◉).

- Fit to screen

- Tile

- Center

⑥ Click **OK**.

⑦ Click the **Close** button (❌).

The picture or color you selected appears on the desktop.

What is the difference between the three Position options?
They differ as follows:

Fit to screen

The Fit to screen option expands the image to fill the entire desktop. This option can distort the image.

Tile

The Tile option repeats your image multiple times to fill the entire desktop.

Center

The center option, which is the Windows Vista default setting, displays the image in the center of the desktop.

Set the Screen Saver

You can set up Windows Vista to display a *screen saver*, a moving pattern or series of pictures. The screen saver appears after your computer has been idle for a while.

If you leave your monitor on for long stretches while your computer is idle, the unmoving image can end up "burned" into the monitor's screen. A screen saver prevents this by displaying a moving image.

Set the Screen Saver

① Open the Personalization window.

Note: See the "Open the Personalization Window" task earlier in this chapter.

② Click **Screen Saver**.

The Screen Saver Settings dialog box appears.

③ Click the **Screen saver** ⏷ and then click the screen saver you want to use.

● A preview of the screen saver appears.

Note: Not all screen savers can display the small preview. To see an actual preview, click **Preview**. When you are done, move the mouse ⏴ or press a key to stop the preview.

④ Click the **Wait** to specify the number of minutes of computer idle time after which the screen saver appears.

⑤ Click **OK**.

The screen saver appears after your computer is idle for the number of minutes you specified in Step **4**.

Note: *To interrupt the screen saver, move the mouse ⍦ or press a key on the keyboard.*

Can I use a screen saver to hide my work while I am away from my desk?
Yes. By itself, the screen saver's pattern automatically obscures the screen. However, another person can interrupt the screen saver to see your work. To prevent this, first assign a password to your Windows Vista user account, as described in the "Protect an Account with a Password" task in Chapter 7. In the Screen Saver tab, make sure you leave the On Resume, Display Welcome Screen check box activated (☑). This means that anyone who interrupts the screen saver can only see your work if he knows your password.

Change the Windows Vista Color Scheme

You can personalize your copy of Windows Vista by choosing a different color scheme, which Vista applies to the window borders, taskbar, and Start menu.

You can also customize the Windows Vista look by toggling the transparent glass effect on and off, setting the color intensity, and even creating your own colors.

Change the Windows Vista Color Scheme

1 Open the Personalization window.

Note: See the "Open the Personalization Window" task earlier in this chapter.

2 Click **Window Color and Appearance**.

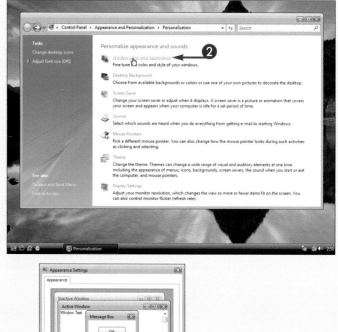

The Appearance Settings dialog box appears.

Note: If you see the Change your color scheme window, instead, skip to Step **6**.

3 In the Color scheme list, click **Windows Vista Aero**.

4 Click **OK**.

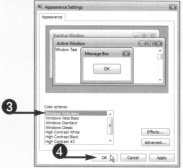

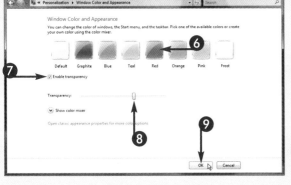

● Windows Vista applies the Aero color scheme and returns you to the Personalization window.

⑤ Click **Window Color and Appearance**.

The Change your color scheme window appears.

⑥ Click the color you want to use.

● Windows Vista changes the color of the window border.

⑦ If you do not want to see the glass effect, click **Enable transparency** (☑ changes to ☐).

⑧ Click and drag the Transparency slider to set the color intensity.

● Windows Vista changes the transparency of the window border.

⑨ Click **OK**.

Windows Vista applies the new color scheme.

My Appearance Settings dialog box does not have the Windows Vista Aero option. Why not?

On systems with lower-end graphics cards or little graphics memory, Windows Vista is unable to display the "glass" interface. On such systems, you choose a standard color scheme instead:

❶ In the Color scheme list, click the color scheme you want to use.

❷ Click **OK**.

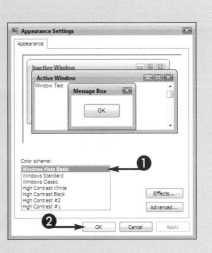

Save a Custom Desktop Theme

After you customize the desktop background, screen saver, and color scheme, you can save all of these changes as a custom desktop theme.

After you save the custom desktop theme, you can reapply it at any time if you make changes in the Personalization window and want to restore your previous look.

Save a Custom Desktop Theme

① Open the Personalization window.

Note: See the "Open the Personalization Window" task earlier in this chapter.

② Click **Theme**.

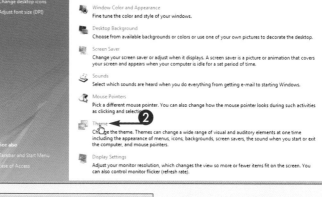

The Theme Settings dialog box appears.

③ Click **Save As**.

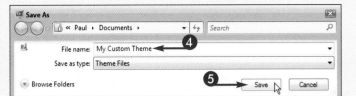

The Save As dialog box appears.

④ Click in the File name text box to type a name for your theme.

⑤ Click **Save**.

● Windows Vista saves your theme.

⑥ Click **OK**.

Note: To reapply your theme later on, follow Steps 1 and 2, click the Theme ⬝, click your saved theme, and then click OK.

Note: To include a custom sound effect in your theme, open the Personalization window and click Sounds. In the Audio Devices and Sound Themes dialog box, click an item in the Program Event list. The program event may be a program closing or a battery alarm. Click a sound effect in the Sounds list, Windows Error for example. Click OK.

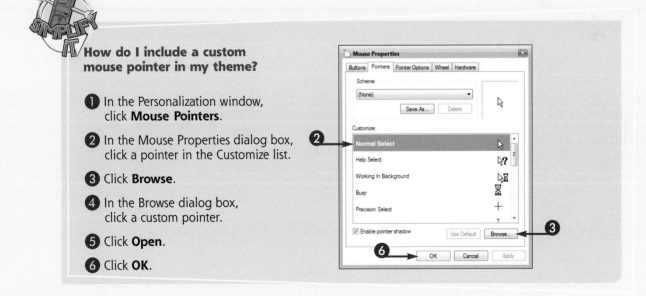

How do I include a custom mouse pointer in my theme?

❶ In the Personalization window, click **Mouse Pointers**.

❷ In the Mouse Properties dialog box, click a pointer in the Customize list.

❸ Click **Browse**.

❹ In the Browse dialog box, click a custom pointer.

❺ Click **Open**.

❻ Click **OK**.

Customize the Start Menu

For example, you can turn off the lists of recently used documents and programs for privacy and you can control the items that appear on the right side of the menu.

You can personalize how the Start menu looks and operates to suit your style and the way you work.

Customize the Start Menu

1 Right-click **Start**.

2 Click **Properties**.

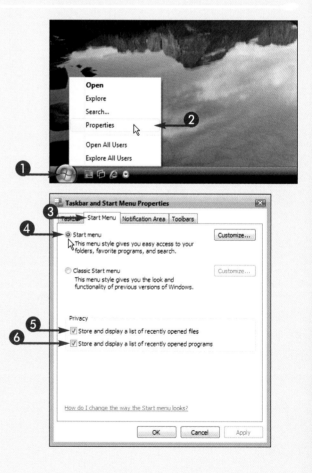

The Taskbar and Start Menu Properties dialog box appears.

3 Click the **Start Menu** tab.

4 Click **Start menu** (⊚ changes to ⊙).

5 If you do not want Windows Vista to list your recently used documents, click here (☑ changes to ☐).

6 If you do not want Windows Vista to list your recently used programs, click here (☑ changes to ☐).

7 Click **Customize**.

The Customize Start Menu dialog box appears.

8 Use the Start menu items list to control the icons that appear on the right side of the Start menu.

● Some items have several option buttons that control how they appear on the Start menu; click the option you want (○ changes to ◉).

● Some items have check boxes that determine whether the item appears (☑) or does not appear (☐) on the Start menu.

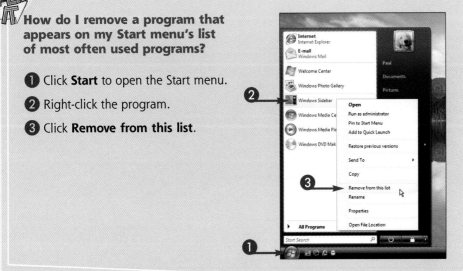

How do I remove a program that appears on my Start menu's list of most often used programs?

1 Click **Start** to open the Start menu.

2 Right-click the program.

3 Click **Remove from this list**.

continued

Customize the Start Menu *(continued)*

To further personalize your Start menu, you can switch to smaller icons to get more items on the menu, can show more of your most often used programs, and can change the Internet and e-mail programs.

Customize the Start Menu *(continued)*

9 To switch to smaller icons, click **Use large icons** (☑ changes to ☐).

10 Click ⬍ to change the maximum number of the most frequently used programs that can appear on the Start menu. (Type a number between 0 and 30; the default value is 8.)

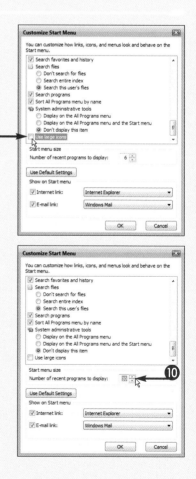

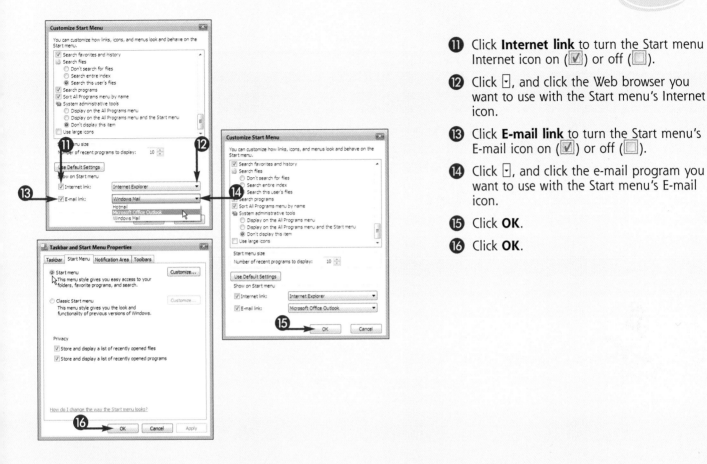

⓫ Click **Internet link** to turn the Start menu Internet icon on (☑) or off (☐).

⓬ Click ⏷, and click the Web browser you want to use with the Start menu's Internet icon.

⓭ Click **E-mail link** to turn the Start menu's E-mail icon on (☑) or off (☐).

⓮ Click ⏷, and click the e-mail program you want to use with the Start menu's E-mail icon.

⓯ Click **OK**.

⓰ Click **OK**.

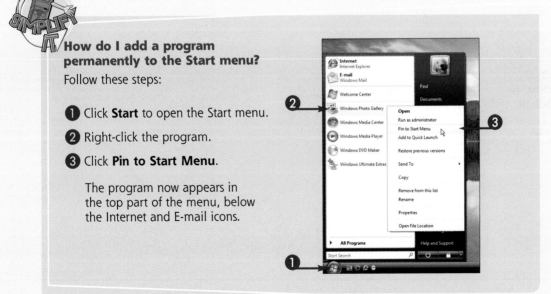

How do I add a program permanently to the Start menu?

Follow these steps:

❶ Click **Start** to open the Start menu.

❷ Right-click the program.

❸ Click **Pin to Start Menu**.

The program now appears in the top part of the menu, below the Internet and E-mail icons.

Customize the Taskbar

You can personalize how the taskbar operates and looks to make it more efficient and suit your working style.

For example, you can unlock the taskbar for moving or resizing, temporarily hide the taskbar, and allow maximized windows to cover the taskbar.

Customize the Taskbar

1 Right-click an empty section of the taskbar.

2 Click **Properties**.

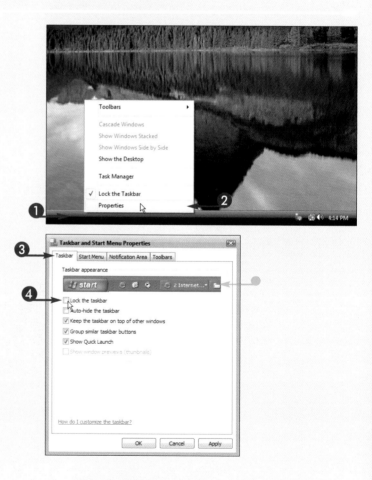

The Taskbar and Start Menu Properties dialog box appears.

3 Click the **Taskbar** tab.

• These areas show you the effect that your changes will have on the taskbar.

4 Click **Lock the taskbar** (☑ changes to ☐) to unlock the taskbar so that you can resize or move it.

Note: To quickly lock and unlock the taskbar, right-click an empty section of the taskbar and click **Lock the taskbar**.

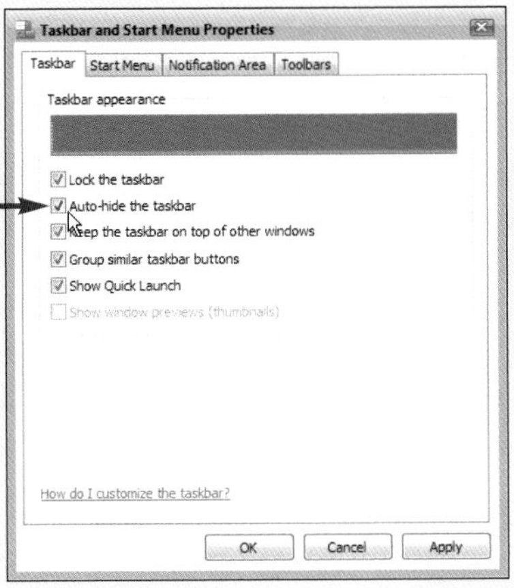

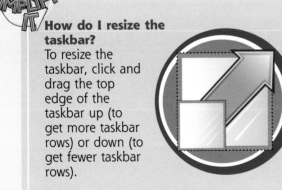

❺ Click **Auto-hide the taskbar** (☐ changes to ☑) to hide the taskbar when you are using a program.

Note: *To display the hidden taskbar, move the mouse to the bottom edge of the screen.*

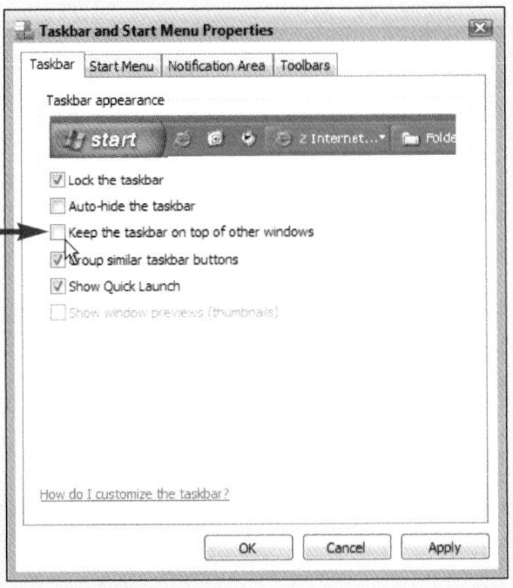

❻ Click **Keep the taskbar on top of other windows** (☑ changes to ☐) to allow maximized windows to use the full screen.

SIMPLIFY IT

How do I resize the taskbar?

To resize the taskbar, click and drag the top edge of the taskbar up (to get more taskbar rows) or down (to get fewer taskbar rows).

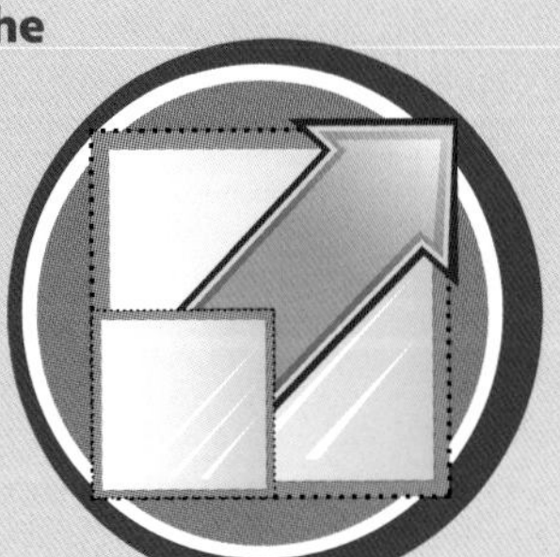

How do I move the taskbar?

To move the taskbar, position the mouse over an empty section of the taskbar, and then click and drag the taskbar to another edge of the screen.

continued

Customize the Taskbar *(continued)*

To further personalize your Start menu, you can group taskbar buttons, show the Quick Launch toolbar, turn off the clock, and reduce the number of icons in the notification area.

Customize the Taskbar *(continued)*

7 Click **Group similar taskbar buttons** (☑ changes to ☐) to disable the grouping of taskbar buttons.

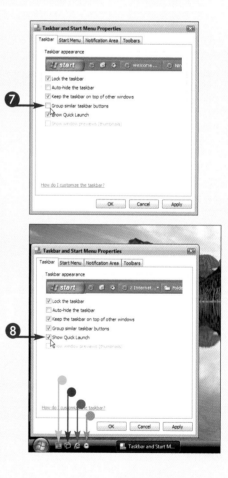

8 Click **Show Quick Launch** (☐ changes to ☑) to display the Quick Launch toolbar.

Quick Launch gives you one-click access to several Windows Vista features.

● Minimizes all open windows.

● Starts Windows Switcher.

● Starts Internet Explorer.

● Starts Windows Media Player.

9 Click the **Notification Area** tab.

10 Click **Hide inactive icons**
(☑ changes to ☐) to display all
the icons in the notification area.

Note: *If you choose to leave the
Hide inactive icons option on, you
can click* ◄ *to display the hidden
icons. Click* ► *again to hide the
icons.*

● If you choose to leave the Hide
inactive icons option on, you can
click the **Show Hidden Icons** icon
(◄) to display the hidden icons.
Click ► again to hide the icons.

11 Use these check boxes to turn
notification area icons on (☑) or
off (☐).

12 Click **OK**.

How do I use the Group Similar Taskbar Buttons feature?

Grouping taskbar buttons
means showing only a
single button for any
program that has
multiple windows
open. To switch to
one of those
windows, click the
taskbar button and
then click the
window name.

How can I control the display of notification area icons?

In the Taskbar and Start Menu Properties
dialog box, click the **Notification Area** tab
and then click **Customize** to display the
Customize Icons
dialog box. For
each icon you
want to work
with, click ▾,
and then click
the behavior
you want: **Hide
when inactive,
Hide,** or **Show**.

Chapter 12

Maintaining Windows Vista

To keep your system running smoothly, maintain top performance, and reduce the risk of computer problems, you need to perform some routine maintenance chores. This chapter shows you how to delete unnecessary files, check for hard drive errors, back up your files, and more.

Check Hard Drive Free Space

If you run out of room on your hard drive, you will not be able to install more programs or create more documents. To ensure this does not happen, you can check how much free space your hard drive has.

Of particular concern is the hard drive on which Windows Vista is installed, usually drive C. If this hard drive's free space gets low — say, less than 20 percent of the total hard drive space — Windows Vista runs slowly.

Check Hard Drive Free Space

① Click **Start**.

② Click **Computer**.

The Computer window appears.

③ Click the drive you want to check.

Note: *You can also check the free space on a CD-ROM, DVD-ROM, memory card, or floppy disk. Before you perform Step 3, insert the disk in the drive.*

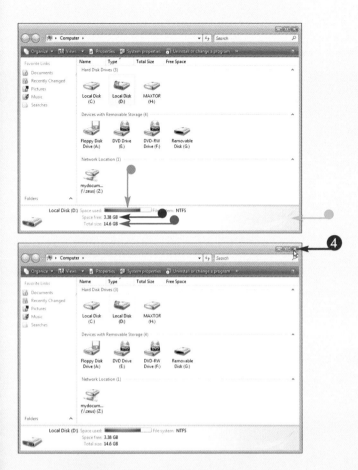

- Information about the disk appears in the Details pane.

- This value tells you the amount of free space on the drive.

- This value tells you the total amount of space on the drive.

- This bar turns red when disk space becomes low.

④ Click the **Close** button (☒) to close the Computer window.

How often should I check my hard drive free space?

With normal computer use, you should check your hard drive free space about once a month. If you install programs, create large files, or download media frequently, you should probably check your free space every couple of weeks.

TIME TO CLEAN UP!

What can I do if my hard drive space is getting low?

You can do three things:

- **Delete Documents.** If you have documents — particularly media files such as images, music, and videos — that you are sure you no longer need, delete them.

- **Remove Programs.** If you have programs that you no longer use, uninstall them (see the "Uninstall a Program" task in Chapter 2).

- **Run Disk Cleanup.** Use the Disk Cleanup program to delete files that Windows Vista no longer uses. See the next task, "Delete Unnecessary Files."

Delete Unnecessary Files

To free up hard drive space on your computer and keep Windows Vista running efficiently, you can use the Disk Cleanup program to delete files that your system no longer needs.

Run Disk Cleanup any time that your hard drive free space gets too low. If hard drive space is not a problem, run Disk Cleanup every two or three months.

Delete Unnecessary Files

① Click **Start**.

② Click **All Programs**.

③ Click **Accessories**.

④ Click **System Tools**.

⑤ Click **Disk Cleanup**.

● The Disk Cleanup Options dialog box appears.

⑥ Click **All files on this computer**.

*Note: You can also click **My files only**, instead, which does not require Administrator-level credentials.*

*Note: If the User Account Control dialog box appears, click **Continue** or type an administrator password and click **Submit**.*

If your computer has more than one drive, the Drive Selection dialog box appears.

⑦ Click the **Drives** ⬝ and then click the hard drive you want to clean up.

⑧ Click **OK**.

Disk Cleanup for (D:)

Disk Cleanup | More Options

You can use Disk Cleanup to free up to 1.14 GB of disk space on (D:).

Files to delete:

☑ 📄 Downloaded Program Files	0 bytes
☑ 📄 Temporary Internet Files	177 KB
☐ 📄 Hibernation File Cleaner	0.99 GB
☐ 📄 Recycle Bin	0 bytes
☐ 📄 Temporary files	0 bytes

Total amount of disk space you gain: 151 MB

Description

Downloaded Program Files are ActiveX controls and Java applets downloaded automatically from the Internet when you view certain pages. They are temporarily stored in the Downloaded Program Files folder on your hard disk.

[View Files]

How does Disk Cleanup work?

⑩ [OK] [Cancel]

Disk Cleanup

Are you sure you want to permanently delete these files?

⑪ [Delete files] [Cancel]

The Disk Cleanup dialog box appears.

● This area displays the total amount of drive space you can free up.

● This area displays the amount of drive space the activated options will free up.

⑨ Click the check box (☐ changes to ☑) for each file type that you want to delete.

● This area displays a description of the highlighted file type.

⑩ Click **OK**.

● Disk Cleanup asks you to confirm that you want to delete the file types.

⑪ Click **Delete files**.

What types of files does Disk Cleanup delete?
It deletes the following file types:

● **Downloaded Program files.** Small Web page programs that are downloaded onto your hard drive.

● **Temporary Internet files.** Web page copies that are stored on your hard drive for faster viewing.

● **Offline Web pages.** Web page copies that are stored on your hard drive for offline viewing.

● **Recycle Bin.** Files that you have deleted since you last emptied your Recycle Bin.

● **Temporary files.** Files used by programs to store temporary data.

● **Thumbnails.** Miniature versions of images and other content used in folder windows.

● **Temporary Offline files.** Local copies of network files.

Defragment Your Hard Drive on a Schedule

You can make Windows Vista, and your programs, run faster, and your documents open more quickly, by defragmenting your hard drive on a regular schedule.

Most files are stored on your computer in several pieces, and over time, those pieces often get scattered around your hard drive. Defragmenting improves performance by bringing all those pieces together, making finding and opening each file faster.

Defragment Your Hard Drive on a Schedule

① Click **Start**.

② Click **All Programs**.

③ Click **Accessories**.

④ Click **System Tools**.

⑤ Click **Disk Defragmenter**.

   Note: If the User Account Control dialog box appears, click **Continue** or type an administrator password and click **Submit**.

The Disk Defragmenter window appears.

⑥ Click **Run automatically (recommended)** (☐ changes to ☑).

⑦ Click **Modify schedule**.

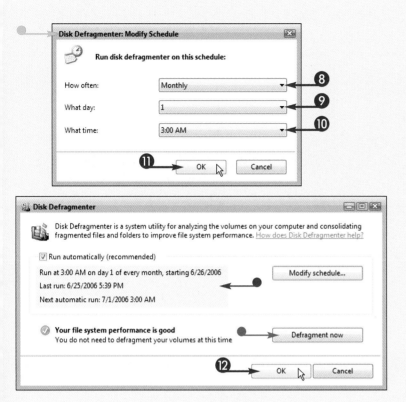

Disk Defragmenter: Modify Schedule

Run disk defragmenter on this schedule:

How often: Monthly ⑧

What day: 1 ⑨

What time: 3:00 AM ⑩

⑪ OK Cancel

Disk Defragmenter

Disk Defragmenter is a system utility for analyzing the volumes on your computer and consolidating fragmented files and folders to improve file system performance. How does Disk Defragmenter help?

☑ Run automatically (recommended)

Run at 3:00 AM on day 1 of every month, starting 6/26/2006

Last run: 6/25/2006 5:39 PM

Next automatic run: 7/1/2006 3:00 AM

Modify schedule...

✓ Your file system performance is good
You do not need to defragment your volumes at this time

Defragment now

⑫ OK Cancel

- The Disk Defragmenter: Modify Schedule dialog box appears.

⑧ Click the **How often** and then click the frequency with which you want to defragment (Daily, Weekly, or Monthly).

⑨ Click the **What day** and click either the day of the week (for a Weekly schedule) or the day of the month (for a Monthly schedule).

⑩ Click the **What time** and then click the time of day to run the defragment.

⑪ Click **OK**.

- The new schedule appears here.

- If you want to defragment your drives now, click **Defragment now**.

⑫ Click **OK**.

How often should I defragment my hard drive?

This depends on how often you use your computer. If you use your computer every day, you should defragment your hard drive weekly. If you use your computer only occasionally, you should defragment your hard drive monthly.

How long will defragmenting my hard drive take?

It depends on the size of the hard drive, the amount of data on it, and the extent of the defragmentation. Budget at least 15 minutes for the defragment, and know that it could take more than an hour.

Check Your Hard Drive for Errors

Because hard drive errors can cause files to become corrupted, which may prevent you from running a program or opening a document, you can use the Check Disk program to look for and fix hard drive errors.

Check Your Hard Drive for Errors

1 Click **Start**.

2 Click **Computer**.

The Computer window appears.

3 Click the hard drive that you want to check.

4 Click **Properties**.

The hard drive's Properties dialog box appears.

5 Click the **Tools** tab.

6 Click **Check Now**.

Note: If the User Account Control dialog box appears, click **Continue** or type an administrator password and click **Submit**.

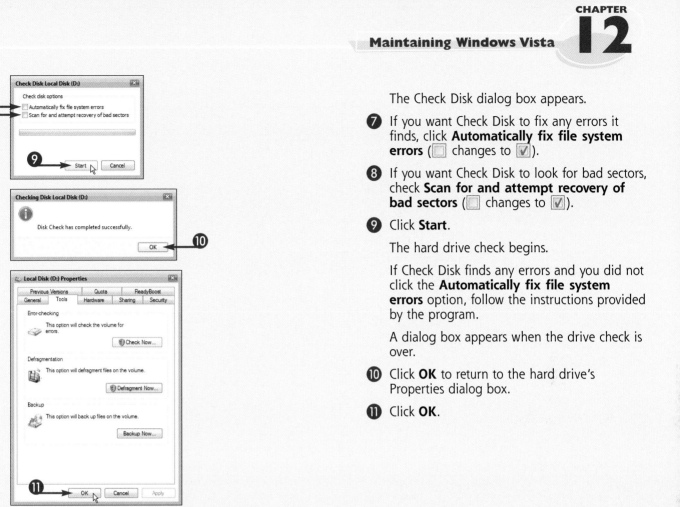

The Check Disk dialog box appears.

7 If you want Check Disk to fix any errors it finds, click **Automatically fix file system errors** (☐ changes to ☑).

8 If you want Check Disk to look for bad sectors, check **Scan for and attempt recovery of bad sectors** (☐ changes to ☑).

9 Click **Start**.

The hard drive check begins.

If Check Disk finds any errors and you did not click the **Automatically fix file system errors** option, follow the instructions provided by the program.

A dialog box appears when the drive check is over.

10 Click **OK** to return to the hard drive's Properties dialog box.

11 Click **OK**.

What is a "bad sector"?
A *sector* is a small storage location on your hard drive. When Windows Vista saves a file on the drive, it divides the file into pieces and stores each piece in a separate sector. A bad sector is one that, through physical damage or some other cause, can no longer be used to reliably store data.

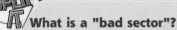

How often should I check for hard drive errors?
You should perform the basic hard drive check about once a week. Perform the more thorough bad sector check once a month. Note that the bad sector check can take several hours, depending on the size of the drive, so only perform this check when you will not need your computer for a while.

Back Up Files

In Windows Vista's Backup program, you can back up to a recordable CD or DVD drive, to another hard drive on your system, or to a network location.

> You can use the Backup program to make backup copies of your important files. If a system problem causes you to lose one or more files, you can restore them from the backup.

Back Up Files

1 Click **Start**.

2 Click **All Programs**.

3 Click **Accessories**.

4 Click **System Tools**.

5 Click **Backup Status and Configuration**.

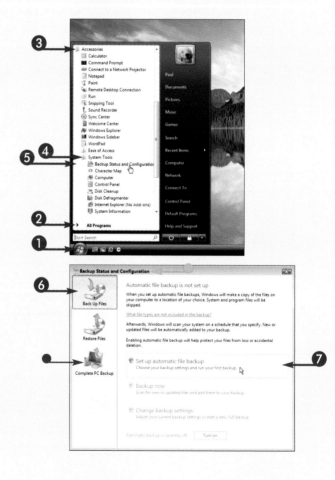

● The Backup Status and Configuration window appears.

6 Click **Back Up Files**.

● If your computer crashes and will no longer start, you can use a CompletePC backup to restore the entire system. CompletePC backup is an exact copy of your entire system. This is called a *system image,* and it includes not only your documents, but also your programs, your Windows Vista configuration, and all the Windows Vista files.

7 Click **Set up automatic file backup**.

> **Note:** If the User Account Control dialog box appears, click **Continue** or type an administrator password and click **Submit**.

The Back Up Files dialog box appears.

⑧ Click **On a hard disk, CD, or DVD** (☐ changes to ✓).

⑨ Click and then click the drive to which you want to back up your files.

Note: *For a recordable CD or DVD drive, be sure to insert a blank disc in the drive.*

● For a network backup, click **On a network** (☐ changes to ✓), click **Browse**, click the network folder, and then click **OK**.

⑩ Click **Next**.

The Which disks do you want to include in the backup dialog box appears.

⑪ If you do not want to include a drive in the backup, click its check box (☐ changes to ✓).

Note: *You cannot uncheck the drive on which Windows Vista is installed.*

⑫ Click **Next**.

I just created some important documents. Can I back up right away?
Yes. First you must complete the steps in this task to perform at least one backup and set your backup configuration. Then follow Steps **1** to **6** to display the Backup Status and Configuration window, and then click **Back up now (A).**

continued

Back Up Files
(continued)

You can use Windows Backup to back up a wide variety of files, including images, music files, videos, and documents.

Note that you only need to run through these configuration steps once. After you have configured your backup schedule, Windows Backup runs automatically.

Back Up Files (continued)

The Which file types do you want to back up dialog box appears.

⑬ If you do not want to include a file type in the backup, click its check box (☐ changes to ☑).

Note: It is best to include all the file types in the backup, just to be safe.

⑭ Click **Next**.

The How often do you want to create a backup dialog box appears.

⑮ Click the **How often** and then click the frequency with which you want to back up (daily, weekly, or monthly).

⑯ Click the **What day** and then click either the day of the week (for a weekly schedule) or the day of the month (for a monthly schedule).

⑰ Click the **What time** and then click the time of day to run the backup.

⑱ Click **Save settings and start backup**.

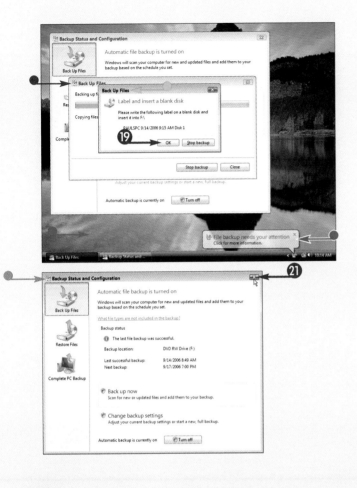

● If you are backing up to a CD or DVD, Windows Backup asks you to insert a blank disc.

⑲ Click **OK**.

● A progress dialog box appears while the program backs up your documents and settings.

● If the medium to which you are backing up becomes full, a pop-up appears.

⑳ Remove the full medium, replace it with a new one, and then click **OK**.

Note: If your backup requires multiple media, you should give each medium a label, such as Backup 1, Backup 2, and so on.

● When the backup is complete, the Backup Status and Configuration window appears.

㉑ Click the **Close** button (❌) to close the window.

How often should I back up my files?

That depends on how often you use your computer and what you use it for. If you use your computer every day to create important business files, then you should consider performing backups daily. If you use your computer only occasionally and do not create many new documents, then you can probably just back up every month. Most people should back up weekly.

Can I change my backup configuration?

Yes. Follow Steps **1** to **6** to display the Backup Status and Configuration window, click **Change backup settings** (●), and then follow Steps **8** to **17** to adjust your configuration. In the final Windows Backup dialog box, click **Save Settings and exit**.

> 🔲 Back up now
> Scan for new or updated files and add them to your backup.
>
> 🔲 Change backup settings
> Adjust your current backup settings or start a new, full backup.

Restore Backed-up Files

You can restore a file from a backup if the file is lost because of a system problem or because you accidentally deleted or overwrote the file.

Restore Backed-up Files

① Click **Start**.

② Click **All Programs**.

③ Click **Accessories**.

④ Click **System Tools**.

⑤ Click **Backup Status and Configuration**.

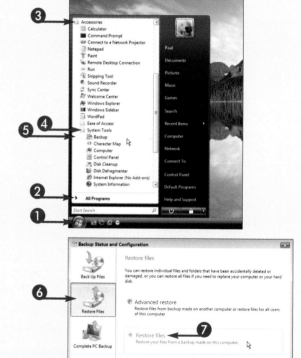

The Backup Status and Configuration window appears.

⑥ Click **Restore Files**.

⑦ Click **Restore files**.

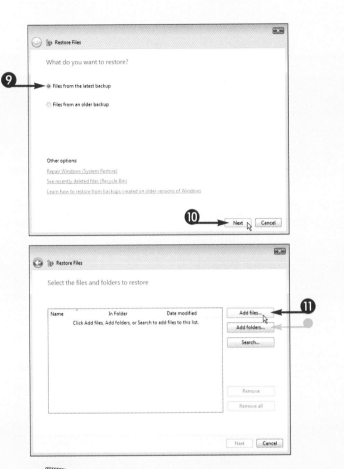

The What do you want to restore dialog box appears.

⑧ If you backed up using a removable medium such as a CD, DVD, or memory card, insert the medium that contains the backups.

⑨ Click **Files from the latest backup** (☐ changes to ☑).

*Note: Windows Backup keeps track of your previous backups and although you will most often want to restore a file from the most recent backup, you can restore files from any stored backup. Click **Files from an older backup** (☐ changes to ☑) and click **Next**. Click the backup you want to use and then click **Next**.*

⑩ Click **Next**.

The Select the files and folders to restore dialog box appears.

⑪ Click **Add files**.

● If you want to restore an entire folder, click **Add folders** instead.

What do I do if I cannot find the file I want to restore?

If you have a large number of files in the backup, it can be difficult to find the one you need. Follow these steps:

❶ Follow Steps **1** to **10** to display the Which files and folders do you want to restore dialog box.

❷ Click **Search**.

● The Search for files to restore dialog box appears.

❸ Use the Search for text box to type some or all of the file name.

❹ Click **Search**.

❺ Click the check box of the file you want to restore (☐ changes to ☑).

❻ Click **Restore**.

Restore Backed-up Files *(continued)*

You can restore all of the backed-up files or you can restore just one or more of the backed-up files.

Restore Backed-up Files *(continued)*

The Add files to restore dialog box appears.

12 Click the folder that contains the files you want to restore.

13 Click the file you want to restore.

Note: *To restore multiple files from the same folder, press and hold and click each file.*

14 Click **Add**.

● The file or files you selected appear in the list.

15 Repeat Steps **11** to **14** to select other files to restore.

16 Click **Next**.

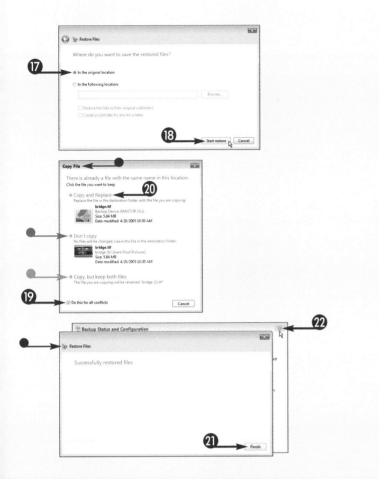

The Where do you want to save the restored files dialog box appears.

17 Click **In the original location** (changes to).

18 Click **Start restore**.

● If a file with the same name exists in the original location, you see the Copy File dialog box.

19 If you want Windows Backup to handle all conflicts the same way, click **Do this for all conflicts** (changes to).

20 Click **Copy and Replace**.

● If you want to keep the original, click **Don't copy** instead.

● If you want to see both files, click **Copy, but keep both files** instead.

● The Successfully restored files dialog box appears.

21 Click **Finish**.

22 Click the **Close** button ( ) to close the Backup Status and Configuration window.

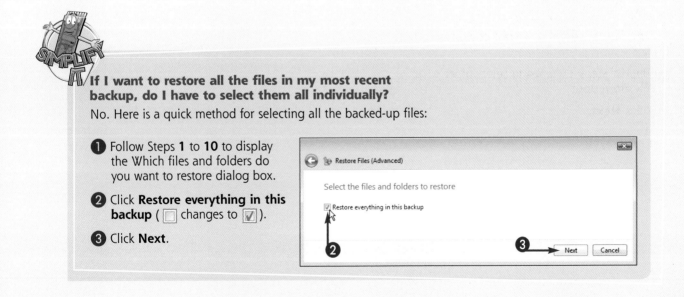

If I want to restore all the files in my most recent backup, do I have to select them all individually?

No. Here is a quick method for selecting all the backed-up files:

1 Follow Steps **1** to **10** to display the Which files and folders do you want to restore dialog box.

2 Click **Restore everything in this backup** (changes to).

3 Click **Next**.

Index

Index

Index